Poison Ivy

This weed (above) causes an itchy rash if you touch it. Poison ivy grows as a vine or shrub. Try to remember what the leaves look like, and do not touch them or other parts of the plant. If you do touch poison ivy, washing your hands as soon as possible may reduce the itching. Your local drugstore will have various remedies that will help.

World Book's

SCIENCE & NATURE GUIDES

MAMMALS

OF THE UNITED STATES AND CANADA

World Book, Inc.
a Scott Fetzer company
Chicago

Scientific names

In this book, after the common name of an organism (life form) is given, that organism's scientific name usually appears. Scientific names are put into a special type of lettering, called italic, *which looks like this.*

The first name in a scientific name is the genus. A genus consists of very similar groups, but the members of these different groups usually cannot breed with one another. The second name given is the species. Every known organism belongs to a particular species. Members of the same species can breed with one another, and the young grow up to look very much like their parents.

An animal's scientific name is the same worldwide. This helps scientists and students to know which animal is being discussed, since the animal may have many different common names.

Therefore, when you see a name like *Eptesicus fuscus,* you know that the genus is *Eptesicus* and the species is *fuscus. Eptesicus fuscus* is the scientific name for the big brown bat (see page 10).

Countryside Code

1 **Always go collecting with a friend,** and always tell an adult where you are going.

2 **Do not touch nests or dens.**

3 **Keep clear of any wild animals that you find**—they may attack you if frightened.

4 **Keep to existing roads, trails, and pathways** wherever possible.

5 **Ask permission** before exploring or crossing private property.

6 **Leave fence gates as you find them.**

7 **Wear long pants, shoes, a hat, and a long-sleeved shirt** in deer tick country.

This edition published in the United States of America by World Book, Inc., Chicago.

WORLD BOOK and the GLOBE DEVICE are registered trademarks or trademarks of World Book, Inc.

World Book, Inc.
233 North Michigan Avenue
Chicago, IL 60601 USA

For information about other World Book publications, visit our Web site **http://www.worldbook.com** or call **1-800-WORLDBK (967-5325).** For information about sales to schools and libraries, call **1-800-975-3250 (United States); 1-800-837-5365 (Canada).**

Copyright © 2007, 2005 Anova Books Company Ltd.
151 Freston Road, London W10 6TH, United Kingdom
www.anovabooks.com

The Library of Congress has cataloged an earlier edition of this title as follows:

Mammals of the United States and Canada.
    p. cm. — (World Book's science & nature guides)
    "Edited text and captions based on Mammals of North America by John Burton"—T.p. verso.
    Includes bibliographical references and index.
    ISBN 0-7166-4215-8 — ISBN 0-7166-4208-5 (set)
    1. Mammals--North America--Juvenile literature. 2. Mammals--North America--Identification--Juvenile literature. I. World Book, Inc. II. Series.
QL715 .M36 2005
599'.097—dc22

                                        2004041962

This edition: ISBN 13: 978-0-7166-4228-2 ISBN 10: 0-7166-4228-X
ISBN 13 (set): 978-0-7166-4221-3 ISBN 10 (set): 0-7166-4221-2

Edited text and captions based on *Mammals of North America* by John Burton. Habitat paintings by Tim Hayward; headbands by Antonia Phillips; and identification and activities illustrations by Mr. Gay Galsworthy.

For World Book:
Editor-in-Chief: Paul A. Kobasa
Editorial: Shawn Brennan, Lisa Kwon, Maureen Liebenson, Christine Sullivan
Research: Mike Barr, Madolynn Cronk, Lynn Durbin, Cheryl Graham, Jacqueline Jasek, Karen McCormack, and Loranne Shields
Librarian: Stephanie Kitchen
Permissions: Janet Peterson
Graphics and Design: Sandra Dyrlund, Isaiah Sheppard
Indexing: Aamir Burki, David Pofelski
Pre-press and Manufacturing: Carma Fazio, Anne Fritzinger, Steven Hueppchen, Madelyn Underwood
Text Processing: Curley Hunter, Gwendolyn Johnson
Proofreading: Anne Dillon

Printed in China
2 3 4 5 6 7 8 9 10 09 08 07 06

Contents

Entries **like this**
indicate pages
featuring
projects you
can do!

Introduction To Mammals

All mammals are warm-blooded and give birth to live young who drink their mother's milk. There are mammals everywhere, in the air and sea, as well as on and under the ground.

This book will help you become more familiar with mammals. It tells you where you are likely to see them and how to recognize some of them. It tells you what signs and tracks they leave behind. Some of the animals in this book are very common and are often seen, like squirrels in city parks or jack rabbits in the countryside. But you will probably only see grizzly bears or beavers in a wildlife park or nature reserve. This book groups the animals according to the habitat, or natural setting, in which they are most common in the wild.

The life of a mammal

Most mammals develop inside their mothers' bodies and are born fully formed. The mother feeds them with her own milk. They rely on their mothers, and sometimes their fathers, too, to look after them until they are strong enough to fend for themselves. Lions, foxes, and other meat-eaters teach their young to hunt Small mammals, such as mice, have several litters each year. Young mice typically stay with their mother for only a few weeks before they leave the nest and build their own.

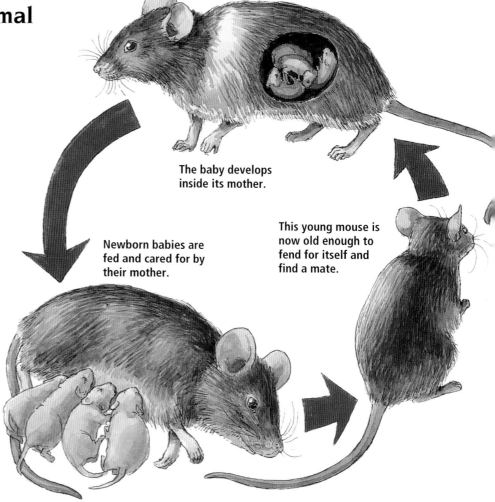

The baby develops inside its mother.

This young mouse is now old enough to fend for itself and find a mate.

Newborn babies are fed and cared for by their mother.

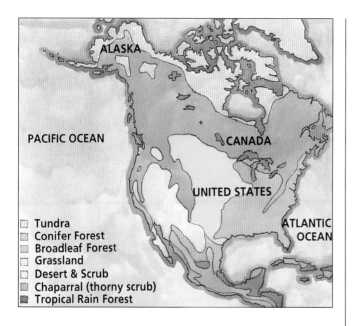

Tundra
Conifer Forest
Broadleaf Forest
Grassland
Desert & Scrub
Chaparral (thorny scrub)
Tropical Rain Forest

Top-of-page Picture Bands

Each habitat has a different picture band at the top of the page. These are shown below.

Found In
Many Habitats

Woods &
Forests

Grasslands
& Savannas

Deserts

Mountains
& Tundras

Rivers &
Waterways

Coasts &
Oceans

How to use this book

To identify a mammal you do not recognize, such as the mammals shown toward the bottom of the page, follow these steps.

1. **Because you will probably get only a brief look at a mammal in the wild,** note the things you noticed about it in your field notebook (see page 31) before trying to identify the animal. Was it big or small? Did it have a long tail? Can you find its tracks to give you additional clues?

2. **Identify which habitat you are in.** There is a description at the start of each section that will help. Each habitat has a different picture band, as shown below, left.

3. **Which of the seven main groups of mammals does it belong to?** Look at pages 6 and 7 to see the main differences between bats, insectivores, rodents, carnivores, ungulates, seals, and whales and dolphins. Mammals from the same group are shown together in each habitat. The rodent shown below is a house mouse (see page 19).

4. **If you can't find the mammal in the first habitat you check,** then look through other habitats. Most mammals are found in more than one kind of habitat. You will find the carnivore shown below (a red fox) on page 13.

5. **If you still can't find the mammal,** you may have to look in a larger field guide.

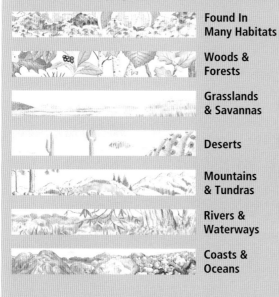

What To Look For

Parts of a mammal

All mammals have fur or hair, except for whales and dolphins. Mammals feed their young with milk and, apart from sea mammals, they all have four limbs. When identifying a mammal, look carefully at:

- the color of its hair or fur
- the shape of its body and head
- the length of its limbs and tail

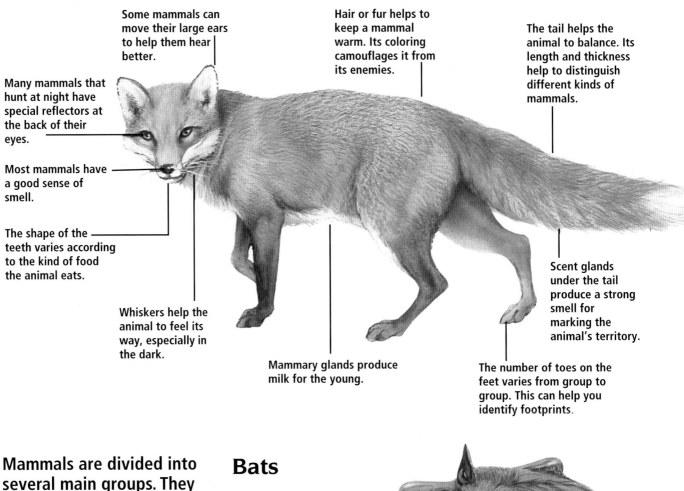

Some mammals can move their large ears to help them hear better.

Many mammals that hunt at night have special reflectors at the back of their eyes.

Most mammals have a good sense of smell.

The shape of the teeth varies according to the kind of food the animal eats.

Whiskers help the animal to feel its way, especially in the dark.

Hair or fur helps to keep a mammal warm. Its coloring camouflages it from its enemies.

The tail helps the animal to balance. Its length and thickness help to distinguish different kinds of mammals.

Scent glands under the tail produce a strong smell for marking the animal's territory.

Mammary glands produce milk for the young.

The number of toes on the feet varies from group to group. This can help you identify footprints.

Mammals are divided into several main groups. They have much the same bones in their bodies, but their length and shape vary according to their lifestyle.

Bats

Bats are the only mammals that can fly. Their wings are made of skin stretched over the bones of their forelimbs. Most bats navigate by sound rather than by sight.

Carnivores

These meat-eaters include lions, foxes, weasels, and bears. Most carnivores have long, sleek bodies and long, strong legs for chasing and pouncing on their prey. They have strong jaws with many sharp teeth for tearing.

Seals

Seals have streamlined, fur-covered bodies and front and back legs in the form of flippers. Seals can swim underwater, but surface to breathe air. They feed at sea, but come ashore to give birth.

Insectivores

They include hedgehogs, moles, and shrews. They all have poor eyesight. Their front limbs are good for digging into the soil. They have small heads and long jaws.

Whales & Dolphins

This group has no back limbs and only short front flippers. Their young are born at sea. All must come to the surface to breathe air. Some whales have teeth, others have baleen plates through which they sift the water for small fish and plankton.

Ungulates

Deer, sheep, goats, and cattle belong to this group. They all have hoofs—these are actually modified toenails. Ungulates have two or more stomach compartments so they can digest tough plants. They often bring partly digested food back into their mouths to chew again—this is called chewing the cud. Instead of sharp, upper teeth many ungulates have a horny pad for chewing leaves and grass. Many ungulates also have horns or antlers.

Rodents

These include mice, rats, gophers, and woodchucks. They have large front teeth for gnawing. Rabbits and hares are closely related to this group.

Found In Many Habitats

There are some mammals that can live almost anywhere. The animals described in this section are so adaptable you may find them in many different habitats. Many wild mammals thrive near people, so look for signs of them in yards, parks, public gardens, and vacant lots.

People have created buildings, yards, parks, and golf courses for their own purposes, not realizing that to animals they resemble natural habitats. Buildings are like rocky cliffs with holes and cracks. Bats can roost in cellars and attics; foxes make their dens under yard sheds, raccoons in chimney flues. Both will feed from garbage cans.

A golf course is much like a clearing in a wood, a well-grazed meadow, or a prairie. Look for signs of deer, moles, rabbits, and skunks here.

Although your home may be surrounded by mammals, they may not be easy to see. You might have to get up very early in the morning to see them.

Many wild animals can be frightened easily, may try to attack you, or may carry disease, so **don't** get near them or touch them. The picture shows eight kinds of mammals from this section. How many can you recognize?

American badger, big brown bat, eastern chipmunk, white-tailed deer, eastern cottontails, northern raccoon, short-tailed weasel, woodchuck.

Found In Many Habitats

Bats are the only mammals that can fly. Their wings are formed by thin skin, which stretches between the very long fingers of their hands. Most bats come out at dusk and are almost impossible to identify as they flit about in the dark. Do not confuse them with birds—they come out after most birds have gone to roost. If you do get a chance to see a bat clearly, look at its ears to help you identify it. In particular, look for the large lobe of skin that guards the entrance to its ears—it is called the tragus and is much more noticeable than in humans. For more about bats, see the activities on page 20.

Eastern Pipistrelle

(Pipistrellus subflavus)
This bat is found only in eastern North America. It is the smallest eastern bat, and its tragus is shorter and blunter than that of other small bats. Its fur is yellowish- to drab-brown. During the summer it roosts mostly in trees and emerges in early evening to look for food. It flies slowly, constantly changing direction. In winter, it usually hibernates in caves and mines.
Bat
Length: 3 in (7.5 cm), of which tail is 1½ in (4 cm)
Feeds on small insects and spiders
Young: usually twins

Little Brown Myotis
(Myotis lucifugus)

The little brown myotis is one of the most common bats in North America and is found almost everywhere, except in Florida, Texas, and southern California. Its fur is brown above and buff below, and its ears are quite long and have a short, rounded tragus. It feeds on flying insects near water or forests, and roosts in buildings near water. The females gather in large colonies (groups) to give birth to their young. In fall, northern bats migrate south to hibernate in caves, mines, and other tunnels.

Bat
Length: 3–3½ in (7.5–9 cm), of which tail is about 1½ in (4 cm)
Feeds on insects
Young: usually 1 baby, very rarely twins

Big Brown Bat

(Eptesicus fuscus)
The big brown bat is another of the most common bats in North America. It is big and brown, although the shade of brown varies from region to region. It has a broad muzzle and rounded ears and tragus. It flies very straight and fast. You are very likely to see this bat around buildings. Look for it near houses, barns, churches, and summer houses. In summer, it gives birth in groups or nurseries of up to 700 bats, but about 150 is more common. In winter it hibernates in buildings.
Bat
Length: 4–5 in (10–12.5 cm), of which tail is almost 2 in (5 cm)
Feeds on insects, particularly large beetles
Young: 1–2 babies

Brazilian Free-tailed Bat

(Tadarida brasiliensis)

This is the most common and widespread free-tailed bat—so called because its tail continues beyond its tail membrane. It is found only in the southern United States, Mexico, and farther south. Its short, thick fur is dark brown or grayish above. It sometimes roosts in buildings, but more often in caves. Thousands, or even a million or more, of these bats gather with their young in nursery roosts. You can tell if you are near one of their roosts by its musky smell. At dusk, so many leave the cave together to feed that from a distance they look like a plume of smoke. They fly high and fast, sometimes traveling several miles (or kilometers) to feed. In winter, most migrate to Mexico up to 1,000 miles (1,600 kilometers) away.

Bat
Length: about 4 in (10 cm), of which tail is 1½ in (4 cm)
Feeds mostly on small moths
Young: 1 baby

Mule Deer

(Odocoileus hemionus)

You may see this deer almost anywhere in the prairies, desert scrub, forests, and mountains of western North America. Its fur is gray or brown. Look for the black tip on its tail to tell it apart from the white-tailed deer. The deer's ears are long and furry like those of a mule and the deer's rump (hind part) is white. Mule deer are most active early in the morning, in the evening, and on moonlit nights. Like many other deer, each buck (male) tries to attract a herd of does (females) in the fall to mate. This is called the rutting season. You can tell the bulls by their antlers, although they lose them in January or February.

Ungulate
Length: 3–6½ ft (91–199 cm), tail is 5–9 in (12–23 cm)
Feeds on herbs and grasses in summer; shrubs, saplings, acorns, and apples in winter
Tracks: 2-toed hoofs
Young: twins

White-tailed Deer

(Odocoileus virginianus)

You may see this deer anywhere in southern Canada and the United States except in the far West. It is similar to the mule deer, but its tail is white underneath and has no black on it, and its ears are smaller. Its coat is reddish-brown in summer and gray in winter. When white-tailed deer are alarmed, they snort and often stick their tails in the air. Only the bucks have antlers. They mate in the fall but, unlike most deer, some bucks mate with only one doe. The fawns are born in the spring and are able to follow their mothers after only a few days. Their fur is heavily spotted. Fully grown deer can run 35 to 40 mph (56 to 64 kph) and jump a gap of up to 30 feet (9 meters).

Ungulate
Length: 4½–6½ ft (137–199 cm), tail is 1 ft (30 cm)
Feeds on grasses, shrubs, trees, and other plants
Tracks: 2-toed hoofs
Young: 1–3 fawns

Short-tailed Weasel

(Mustela erminea)

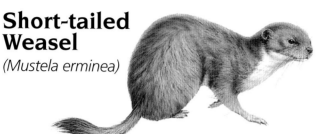

Carnivore: Weasel family
Length: 7–13 in (18–33 cm), tail is 1½–3½ in (2.5–9 cm)
Feeds mainly on mice and voles, but also eats birds, shrews, and young rabbits
Tracks: 4 toes with central pad—Young: 1 litter of 3–13 babies per year

Short-tailed weasels are found in most of Canada, near the Great Lakes, and in the United States in Alaska and the northeastern and northwestern reaches of the lower 48 states. In summer, they are brown on top and white underneath. In winter, many northern animals become white all over except for the black tip on their tails. They are also called ermines and were sometimes hunted for their white winter fur. Short-tailed weasels are most active at night and hunt mainly on the ground. They climb trees to prey on nesting birds. Listen for their shrill shriek as they seize their prey. They dig a burrow under rocks, tree stumps, or old buildings.

American Badger

(Taxidea taxus)

Badgers are found from the western United States to the Great Lakes, and in southwestern Canada. They are most active at night, but you may see one beside the highway early in the morning. You will easily recognize one from its stout, squat body, small head, white stripe from nose to shoulders, and white-and-black head and face markings. Badgers have long, strong claws, which they use for digging out prey and dens for shelter. You can tell a badger's den by the pile of excavated soil in front.

Carnivore: Weasel family
Length: 20–35 in (51–89 cm), tail is 4–6 in (10–15 cm)
Feeds mainly on small mammals, such as ground squirrels, prairie dogs, gophers, mice, and rodents, but also snakes and insects
Tracks: 5 toes with long claws and central pad
Young: 1 litter of 1–5 babies

Long-tailed Weasel

(Mustela frenata)

Long-tailed weasels are found in southern Canada and over most of the United States, except for the extreme southwest. They look like short-tailed weasels except that they are bigger, and their tails are longer. Males are much larger than females. They are most active at night, and live in any kind of habitat, provided it is close to water. Although they spend most time on the ground, they do climb trees to prey on birds. They make nests under piles of wood or rocks, often in the abandoned burrows of other animals. In winter their coats turn completely white.

Carnivore: Weasel family
Length: 12–22 in (30–56 cm), tail is 3–6 in (8–15 cm)
Feeds on small mammals, including rabbits and squirrels, and birds, including poultry
Tracks: 4 toes with central pad
Young: 1 litter of 4–8 babies

Red Fox
(Vulpes fulva)

Red foxes are sleek, slender animals that look much like small dogs. Their fur is rusty-red or red-orange on top and white below, and their long, bushy tails have a white tip. Look for them in woods or forests throughout northern North America. Also, they can be seen in the wooded areas of suburbs of towns, golf courses, and cemeteries. They are most active at night, but you may see one in the early morning. Listen at night for their drawn-out, high-pitched barking. Red foxes may sleep out in the open, but they dig a den in sloping ground for their litters (young). Look for fox droppings. They often contain fur, feathers, and broken bones—the parts of their prey they could not digest.

Carnivore: Dog family
Length: 23–27 in (58–69 cm),
tail is 14–16 in (36–41 cm)
Feeds on small mammals,
birds, fruit, and insects
Tracks: 4 toes and pad
Young: usually 1 litter
of 4–9 cubs

Gray Fox
(Urocyon cinereoargenteus)

Gray foxes are found in far southern Canada and throughout most of the United States and Mexico. They are similar in shape to a red fox, but their fur is grizzled gray on top with an orangy band around the sides. Their underparts are white. The gray fox is a secretive animal and is most active at night. It likes to live where there are plenty of trees or scrubby bushes and will climb into a tree to escape from danger. It builds a den in a hollow tree, thicket, or under a boulder.

Carnivore: Dog family
Length: 23–27 in (58–69 cm),
tail is 14–16 in (36–41 cm)
Feeds on small mammals, birds, insects, and fruit
Tracks: 4 toes and pad
Young: usually 1 litter of 3–5 cubs

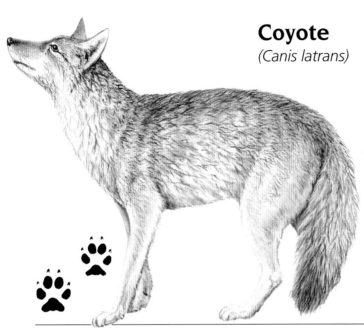

Coyote
(Canis latrans)

Coyotes are larger than foxes and smaller than wolves, but they look similar to both. They are easily confused with dogs. Coyotes are very adaptable and can live in mountains, deserts, and even in the center of cities. You may see them anywhere in North America, except in the extreme north. They are most active at night. Listen for them howling and "yipping" at dusk and dawn. They are true scavengers and will eat almost anything they find.

Carnivore: Dog family
Length: 4 ft (1.2 m), tail is 11–16 in (28–41 cm)
Feeds on mammals such as sheep, deer, and rabbits. Also feeds on poultry, frogs, and all kinds of dead animals
Tracks: 4 toes with central pad
Young: 1 litter of 5–6 pups

Northern Raccoon
(Procyon lotor)

Raccoons are one of the best-known carnivores in North America. You cannot miss their black-ringed tails and the black mask of fur around their eyes. You may see them near the highway throughout southern Canada and the United States, except for the highest parts of the Rockies. They are most active at night but can be seen during the day. Raccoons will eat almost anything. In cities, they live in storm drains and raid garbage cans. In the country, they like to feed along streams and lakes. They make a den in a hollow tree or in a crack in the rocks, or may dig a burrow. When it gets very cold, they become sleepy, or sluggish, but they do not hibernate.

Carnivore: Raccoon family
Length: 24–42 in (61–107 cm), of which tail is 8–16 in (20–41 cm)
Feeds on all kinds of food, including fruit, crabs, frogs, fish, birds, insects, and rodents
Tracks: 5 toes
Young: usually 1 litter of 3–4 babies

Brown Rat

(Rattus norvegicus)

A brown rat's fur is grayish-brown, with a greasy sheen. Its tail is like the black rat's tail, only shorter. Brown rats, also called Norway rats, probably came originally from Siberia and China and were brought to North America in ships. They are common in cities, farms, and wherever there are people. In some cities, brown rats outnumber people. They live in sewers, and burrow under garbage dumps and along the foundations of buildings. They live in colonies and are active mainly at night. Be careful: brown rats are pests that carry the germs of several diseases.

Rodent
Length: 8–10 in (20–25.5 cm) excluding tail
Feeds on almost anything
Tracks: 4 toes on front feet, 5 on back feet
Young: up to 6 litters, each with 8–9 pups

Black Rat
(Rattus rattus)

Rodent
Length: 7–8 in (18–20 cm)
Feeds on anything it can find
Tracks: 4 toes on front feet, 5 on back feet
Young: usually 3–6 litters a year, each with 6–7 pups

Black rats originally lived in Asia. They reached Europe overland or on ships. From Europe they spread to North America by ship. Although they are most common around ports, especially in the Gulf states, they have spread to some inland cities and farm areas. They are usually found only where there are people. They damage foods stored in such places as warehouses and barns. They climb well, up both trees and buildings. They have black, smoky-gray, or grayish-brown fur, and a long, scaly tail. Be careful: black rats are pests that carry the germs of several diseases.

Bobcat
(Lynx rufus)

Bobcats are found across southern Canada and most of the United States, except the Midwest. They are medium sized with thick, yellow-brown fur above, flecked with black. They have tufted ears and ruffs of fur on the sides of the face. They have short tails, and can be confused with a Canadian lynx (see page 26). Bobcats can adapt to many kinds of habitats.

They are most active at twilight and are seldom seen. Look for their tracks instead. Bobcats make a den in a hollow tree or a crack in the rocks.

Carnivore: Cat family
Length: 24–25 in (61–114 cm)
Feeds on small mammals and birds
Tracks: 4 toes with central pad

Mountain Lion
(Felis concolor)

Mountain lions also are called cougars, pumas, catamounts, and panthers. They are easy to recognize with their buff-colored coats and lion-like faces. They like wild country, such as mountains, marshes, and forests, and may be found in most of western North America, with a few in the Appalachians and in Florida. You are most likely to see one where there are plenty of deer. It makes its den in a cave or other sheltered place among the rocks and marks its territory with scrapes (piles of twigs, grass, and other material).

Carnivore: Cat family
Length: 5 ft (1.5 m), tail is 2–3 ft (61–91 cm)
Feeds mostly on mammals, such as deer, beaver, porcupines, rabbits, sheep and, rarely, domestic animals
Tracks: 4 toes with central pad
Young: a litter of 1–5 cubs every second year

Found In Many Habitats

Southern Flying Squirrel
(Glaucomys volans)

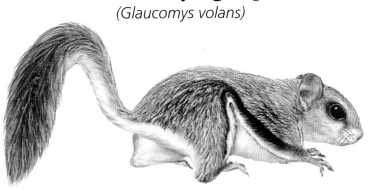

This tiny squirrel has thick, silky fur which is gray on top and white below. Down each side of its body, it has a fold of loose skin that stretches between its front and back legs and allows it to glide from tree to tree. Although southern flying squirrels are found all over the eastern United States, they are not often seen because they are active only at night. They hoard food for the winter. They do not hibernate, but stay in their nests in old woodpecker holes, in bird boxes, or in house attics during bad weather.

Rodent: Squirrel family
Length: 8–9½ in (20–24 cm), of which nearly half is the tail
Feeds on seeds, nuts, berries, insects, and carrion
Young: usually 2 litters, each with 2–3 babies

American Pygmy Shrew

(Sorex hoyi)
The American pygmy shrew is the smallest mammal in North America. It is found throughout most of Canada, parts of the northern United States, and in the Appalachians. You can tell it is a shrew by its long, pointed nose and small, beady eyes. Like all shrews, its ears are almost totally hidden in its fur. It is a very busy little animal, and is active both day and at night, but it is seldom seen. Look among leaf litter (leaves on the forest floor) and grass for their tiny tunnels, no more than an inch (or 2.5 centimeters) wide.

Insectivore
Length: 2½–4½ in (6–11 cm), of which tail is about 1 in (2.5 cm)
Feeds on insects, their larvae, and worms
Young: probably several litters, each with 3–8 babies

Eastern Mole
(Scalopus aquaticus)

The eastern mole is found from Massachusetts and Florida to Texas. This small gray or brown animal lives most of its life underground, so you will be lucky to see one. It has broad front feet for digging through the soil and, because it hardly ever needs to see, tiny eyes which are covered with thick skin or fur. As it builds its tunnels it pushes out the loose soil from time to time, making molehills. Some of the tunnels are as much as 2 feet (61 centimeters) below the surface, but if you see a line of broken grass and soil, you will know there is a tunnel close to the surface. Moles are active both day and night, and all through the winter. They love vegetable gardens.

Insectivore
Length: 5–8 in (13–20 cm) including 1 in (2.5 cm) tail
Feeds mainly on earthworms—Young: 1 litter of 2–5 babies

Western Chipmunk
(Eutamias)

There are more than 12 species of western chipmunk. They tend to be slightly smaller than the eastern chipmunk and vary in color from browns to grays. They all have different patterns of black-and-white stripes on their backs and faces, and are difficult to tell apart.

Rodent: Squirrel family
Length: 6½–12½ in (16.5–32 cm),
of which tail is 2½–5½ in (6–14 cm)
Feeds on seeds and other plant material, also insects
Tracks: 4 toes on front feet, 5 toes on back feet
Young: 1 or 2 litters, each with 2–7 babies

You can recognize a chipmunk by its bushy tail, big ears, and striped back. When it runs, it holds its tail straight up. Eastern chipmunks are found in the east from southeastern Canada to northern Florida. They are reddish-brown with a dark stripe down the middle of their backs, and a white stripe between two black stripes on each side. The underside is gray or white. The best place to look for them is in open woodland. Listen for their chip and chuck calls. Chipmunks fill their cheek pouches with food until they are full, then take the food back to their burrows. They dig their own burrows under the ground with a chamber for storing food. They sleep at night and are active during the day. In winter, they hibernate, waking occasionally to feed.

Eastern Chipmunk
(Tarnias striatus)

Rodent: Squirrel family
Length: 8½–12 in (22–30 cm), of which tail is 3–4 in (8–10 cm)
Feeds on nuts, seeds, and plant material, also snails and insects
Tracks: 4 toes on front feet, 5 toes on back feet
Young: 2 litters of 2–8 babies

Striped Skunk (Mephitis mephitis)

This is one of the best-known mammals in the United States and Canada. It is black with broad white stripes down its back. Its white fur begins as a narrow white stripe up its forehead, broadens into a white band on its neck, then divides into two broad stripes. It lives in deserts, woods, farms, and even yards. It hunts mainly at night, and digs a den in the ground, under abandoned buildings, boulders, or piles of wood. It does not hibernate, but several females may share a den in winter. Keep away from skunks so you will not be sprayed with their bad-smelling defensive liquid.

Carnivore: Weasel family
Length: 13–18 in
(33–46 cm) excluding tail
Feeds mostly on insects,
small mammals, and eggs,
as well as fruit, plants, and carrion
Tracks: 5 toes with central pad
Young: 1 litter of 4–5 babies

Eastern Cottontail
(Sylvilagus floridanus)

The eastern cottontail is the most common wild rabbit in eastern North America. You will also see it in parts of the southwestern United States. It is easy to recognize from its long ears, long back legs, and short, cottony, white tail. Its fur is brownish above and white below. It feeds from early evening until dawn. Look for its droppings where it has been feeding. Most cottontails do not burrow, but hide during the day in a slight dip in the ground close to thick grass or a fallen log for extra cover. When she is ready to give birth, the female digs a nest and lines it with her fur.
Rabbit family
Length: 21½ in (55 cm)
Feeds on grasses in summer; twigs and shoots in winter
Tracks: 4 toes surrounded by foot
Young: 3–4 litters, each with 4–5 babies

Eastern Gray Squirrel

(Sciurus carolinensis)
Gray squirrels are very well known in eastern North America from southern Canada to eastern Texas. Look for the long, bushy tail, gray upper fur, and white underparts. You will see them in woods, parks, or yards. Many build a winter nest in a tree hole or a summer nest of leaves in the branches. Although they come down to the ground, they never stay far from a tree. They are active during the day, even in winter. In fall, you may notice a gray squirrel hiding acorns and nuts one at a time in the ground. Many of these buried nuts are never retrieved—they may grow into new trees.
Rodent: Squirrel family
Length: 17–19 in (43–48 cm), of which tail is about half
Feeds on nuts, berries, buds, bark, and eggs
Tracks: 4 toes on front feet, 5 toes on back feet
Young: 1 or 2 litters, each with 4–8 babies

Golden Mouse

Rodent: Length: 5½–7½ in (14–19 cm), of which tail is nearly half
Feeds on seeds mostly, but also other plant material and insects
Tracks: 4 toes on front feet, 5 toes on back feet
Young: usually several litters, each with 2–3 babies

(Ochrotomys nuttalli)
You can tell this from the deer mouse by its beautifully colored fur: bright golden-cinnamon on top, with white below. The golden mouse is found in many habitats, but only in the southeastern United States. It makes its home in boulder-strewn hillsides, trees, vines, and in brush, and wraps its tail around stalks and twigs to help it climb. It makes a nest of leaves and shredded bark, and may share it with other mice. It is most active at night.

Woodchuck

(Marmota monax)

Woodchucks are also known as ground hogs. They are found across Canada and in part of Alaska and the northeastern and midwestern United States, in woods, meadows, and fields. A woodchuck has a stocky body, short legs, small ears, and a bushy tail. Its brownish fur is grizzled with gray. Listen for its whistle when it is alarmed, and for its growls and chatters when disturbed. Although they come aboveground for only an hour or two each day, you are very likely to see one in the later afternoon, sunning itself near the entrance to its burrow. They usually dig their burrow near those of other woodchucks, and each burrow may have several entrances. Woodchucks hibernate during the winter.

Rodent: Squirrel family
Length: 16–32 in (40–81 cm), of which tail is 4–9 (10–21 cm)
Feeds on grasses, clover, and other plants
Tracks: 4 toes on front feet, 5 toes on back feet
Young: 1 litter of 4–5 babies

Deer Mouse

(Peromyscus maniculatus)

You can tell this is a mouse by its large ears and eyes, and long tail. It can be seen over most of North America in all kinds of habitat from deserts to wet woodlands. Its fur varies in color from dark brown to gray above, and white below. Most active at night, it stores its uneaten food. It makes the largest stores in fall. It builds its nest in a hole in the ground or a tree, or in buildings.

Rodent
Length: 6–8 in (15–20 cm),
tail 2½–4 in (6–10 cm)
Feeds on nuts, berries, seeds, and insects
Tracks: 4 toes on front feet, 5 toes on back feet
Young: up to 4 litters or more, each with 1–9 babies

House Mouse

Rodent
Length: 5–7 in (13–18 cm), of which half is the tail
Feeds outside mostly on seeds, including grain; inside, anything humans eat
Tracks: 4 toes on front feet, 5 toes on back feet
Young: up to 13 litters, each with 4–7 babies

(Mus musculus)
Some house mice live outside in open scrub, but most prefer to live in and around houses and farm buildings. The house mouse is probably the best-known rodent over most of North America. Its fur is dull gray-brown above, and yellowish below. A deer mouse has a white underside. House mice living outside are most active at night. The first sign that there are mice in your house will probably be their small black droppings in a cupboard or place where there is food. They will eat almost anything, and can do a lot of damage in grocery stores.

Encouraging Bats

Most bats roost during the day by hanging upside down in a dark, quiet place. Many roost in trees, mine shafts, and caves. But as these are cut down or filled in, some roost in buildings instead. If you want to encourage them to come around your house, put up a few bat boxes (see right).

Around the house

The picture shows how bats can get into your house and where they may be roosting. You will probably not even know they are there. Some are so small that they can creep through cracks and holes as narrow as ¾ inch (2 centimeters) wide.

If you see bats flying around your house at dusk, look for bat droppings in the attic or on a window sill. (They look like mouse droppings, but are crumbly.) If you think you have found a roost, do not disturb it. Call your local bat group for information and assistance.

Bats and their roosts

You should not disturb bats or their roosts (the places where they rest and sleep). During the year bats use several different roosts. In summer, mothers may group together to give birth and to look after their babies. Many may cram into a tight space to keep each other warm. In winter, bats may fly many miles (or kilometers) away to find roosts that will provide just the right temperature for hibernating.

Bats will roost in almost any part of a roof. They are unlikely to come into the attic space at all, but if they do, put a sheet under their roost to catch their droppings.

Finding their way

Most animals that hunt at night have large eyes to see in the dark, but some bats use their ears instead. When such a bat flies, it makes high-pitched squeaks. The bat listens for the echoes as these sounds bounce off objects around it. This activity is called echolocation, and it helps the bat tell the shape of things and how close they are. Most of the sounds that bats make are much too high-pitched for humans to hear.

Make a bat house

8 in (20 cm)	4 in (10 cm)	6 in (15 cm)	15 in (38 cm)	4 in (10 cm)	8 in (20 cm)
Roof	Base	Front	Back Plate	Side	Side

1 **Buy a piece of wood** that is at least 45 in (114 cm) long, 6 in (15 cm) wide, and 1 in (2.5 cm) thick. Make sure it has not been treated with wood preservative because that is poisonous to bats.

Where to hang the bat house

Your bat house should be at least 10 feet (3 meters) above the ground. Ask an adult to help you position it as high as you safely can on the south side of a tree in a sunny location, or on your house. The best time to put up your bat house is in spring.

The more bat houses you can put up, the better chance you have of attracting bats, but you must be patient. It may take several months for a bat to find your bat house. If you have no luck after a year, move the bat house somewhere else.

2 **Ask an adult to saw the wood into pieces,** as shown above.
3 **Scratch the wood for the back plate with a nail** so that it is rough enough for the bats to hang on to with their claws.
4 **Nail the sides to the front** so that the sides slope down to the front.
5 **Now nail the base to the sides and front.**
6 **Nail the sides to the back.** There should be a slit about 2 in (5 cm) wide between the base and the back.
7 **Nail the roof to the wall tops.**
8 **Nail a piece of roofing felt over the joint** between the back plate and the roof to stop water from getting in.

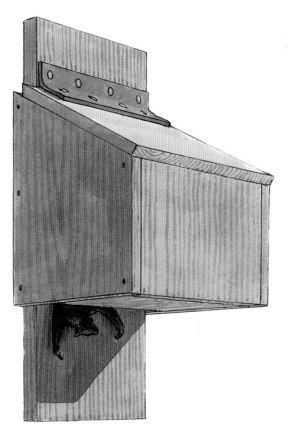

Woods & Forests

There are many different kinds of forests in North America. For example, deciduous forests cover an area from the coastal plains of the eastern and southern United States to the Great Lakes in the north and the Great Plains in the west. Mountain evergreen forests grow above the mountain foothills of the western United States and Canada.

Trees once covered most of North America east of the Mississippi River, but by 1900 settlers had cleared most of the land as far north as New England. The forests which grow there now are new forests. Many native mammals depended on the original mix of trees. Some have disappeared altogether, while others, such as bats, are now much rarer.

Natural forests provide a much wider range of habitats. Mixed woods are good places for animals to live. They can make a nest or den among the shrubs, under the ground, or high in the trees. Bats roost in tree holes and hollow trees. Rodents feed on berries and nuts. Pine martens, lynx, and other carnivores prey on the rodents.

It is often difficult to spot woodland mammals during the day because many of them are active primarily at night. Clearings where a large tree has fallen, and woodland streams are good places to look for tracks, fur, partly eaten food, and droppings. Look in older trees, too, for holes which open into animal homes. The picture shows nine mammals from this book. How many can you recognize?

Red bat, American elk, snowshoe hare, Canadian lynx, American marten, Virginian opossum, North American porcupine, Eastern fox squirrel, gray wolf.

Red Bat
(Lasiurus borealis)

Red bats get their name from their brick-red fur, which is much brighter in the males than the females. Both have white patches on their shoulders and white tips on their backs and bellies. They are found over most of eastern North America and in the extreme West and Southwest. They roost in tree holes and behind bark, or you may see one hanging among the leaves. Red bats live on their own, and are difficult to see because they do not emerge from their roosts until it is nearly completely dark. They hunt over trees, flying fast, but steadily. The northernmost groups migrate south in the fall.

Bat
Length: 3½–5 in (9–13 cm), of which tail is 2–2½ in (5–6 cm)
Feeds on insects
Young: usually 2–4 babies

Silver-haired Bat
(Lasionycteris noctivagans)

You can see these bats in most of the United States and southern Canada. A silver-haired bat will come out fairly early in the evening, and hunt on its own. Look for it flying slowly, high above the trees. It gets its name from the silver tips which give its almost black fur a frosted look. It roosts under the bark of trees and in woodpecker holes. They sometimes collide with very tall buildings and radio towers. In winter, they migrate south, possibly in groups, to hibernate. They usually hibernate under bark, but some do hibernate in caves and mines.

Bat—Length: 3½–4 in (9–10 cm), of which tail is about 1 in (2.5 cm)
Feeds on moths, flies, and other flying insects
Young: twins

Moose
(Alces alces)

The moose is the largest deer in the world. The top of a male's shoulders is over 6 feet (2 meters) high, and it can weigh 800–1,400 lbs (360–640 kg). Females are much smaller and weigh less. Males have huge, flat antlers up to 6 feet (2 meters) across, which they shed in winter. Look for the long flap of skin that hangs from their throats. Moose are found across most of Canada and south through the Rockies. They may be seen at any time of the day, although they are most active at night. Listen for the loud, bellowing calls that bulls (males) and cows (females) make during their mating season in the fall.

Ungulate
Height: 6½ ft (2 m) at the shoulder
Feeds on leaves of willows, aspen, birch, and other trees that grow near water
Tracks: 2-toed hoofs
Young: 1–3 calves

Townsend's Big-eared Bat
(Corynorhinus townsendii)

Townsend's big-eared bat has enormous ears—up to 1½ inches (4 cm) long. When it is resting it folds them back over its neck or coils them like rams' horns, and unfurls them when it is disturbed. This bat is common in the West, but it is endangered in the East where there are scattered populations to Virginia. They emerge after dusk, and hover over the trees picking off moths. In June, the females form colonies of up to 1,000 bats to give birth to their young, and remain together to look after

Bat
Length: 3½–4 in (9–10 cm), of which tail is 1½–2 in (4–5 cm)
Feeds on moths and other insects
Young: 1 baby

them. In winter, they again form large colonies to hibernate in caves, tightly packed together. (For more about bats, see pages 10 and 20-21.)

Mountain Beaver
(Aplodontia rufa)

A mountain beaver does not always live in mountains, and is not closely related to beavers. It is somewhat smaller than a rabbit, and is brownish-black with small eyes and short, rounded ears. It has short legs and almost no tail. It lives in wet forests close to streams from British Columbia to northern California. Mountain beavers are most active at night, and build long burrows into the banks of streams. The entrance to their burrows can be up to 18 inches (46 cm) across. In very wet places, they cover the entrance with twigs, leaves, and ferns up to 2 feet (61 cm) high.
Rodent—Length 12 in (30 cm), of which tail is 2 in (5 cm) or less
Feeds on bark, twigs, berries, and pine needles
Tracks: 5 toes, webbed back feet
Young: 1 litter of 2–3 babies

Virginian Opossum
(Didelphis virginiana)

Opossums are the only marsupials (animals that carry their young in a pouch) in North America. The new-born young are tiny—the whole litter could fit in a tablespoon. The babies crawl into their mother's pouch and develop there for about two months. When the young opossums leave their mother's pouch, they often travel on her back, gripping her tail with their own tail. Opossums are found in woods near fields in the eastern United States, and have been introduced on the West Coast. You are most likely to see them on highways. An opossum has a pointed, white face and grizzled, grayish fur. Its tail has few hairs.
Marsupial
Length: 2–3 ft (61–95 cm), of which tail is 9–21 in (23–53 cm)
Feeds on fruit, vegetables, nuts, meat, eggs, insects, and carrion
Tracks: 5 toes spread wide
Young: usually 2 litters, each up to 20 babies

Gray Wolf
(Canis lupus)

Gray wolves, a name that also refers to timber wolves and tundra wolves, used to roam over most of North America, but are now found only in Canada and the United States in Alaska and around the Great Lakes. You will probably have to go to a very remote place to hear their long, deep howl. A gray wolf looks similar to a coyote (see page 14), but it is larger and its bark is less yappy. The color of its fur usually is gray but may be anything from white to yellow to reddish-brown to almost black. Wolves live in packs of about eight and hunt mainly at dusk, night, and early morning. The strongest male leads the pack.

Carnivore: Dog family
Length: 5–6½ ft (1.5–2 m), including tail
Feeds mostly on mammals, including moose and caribou
Tracks: 4 toes with central pad
Young: 1 litter usually of 1–11 pups

Canadian Lynx
(Lynx canadensis)

Lynxes look much like bobcats (see page 15), and are easily confused with them. Lynxes, however, are found farther north, from Alaska to Newfoundland and Labrador. It is mainly around the U.S. border and the U.S. Rockies that the two species overlap. You will have to look carefully to see that a lynx has bigger ear tufts and a black tip to its short tail. Lynxes like thick forests where they hunt alone and mainly at night. They have very large feet and leave big tracks in the snow. They build a den in a hollow log, under roots, or other sheltered places.

Carnivore: Cat family
Length: 2–3½ ft (61–107 cm), of which tail is 2–5½ in (5–14 cm)
Feeds on mammals, particularly snowshoe hares, and birds
Tracks: 4 toes with central pad
Young: 1 litter of 1–4 kittens

American Marten
(Martes americana)

You can tell this is a weasel from its long, lithe body, short legs, and long, bushy tail. Its fur is a dark glossy brown or yellowish-brown, with a buff or orange patch on its throat and chest. It lives mainly in conifer forests, throughout most of Canada and south into the U.S. Rockies and New England. American martens are most active at night and spend much of their time hunting in trees, but they come down to the ground to forage for food. Their tracks are clearest in early spring and summer. In winter, their feet are covered in thick hair, and this tends to blur their footprints. They make a den in a hollow tree or log.

Carnivore: Weasel family
Length: 20–25 in (51–64 cm), of which tail is 5½–9 in (14–23 cm)
Feeds on small mammals, birds, insects, and fruit
Tracks: 5 toes
Young: 1 litter of 1–5 babies

Fisher
(Martes pennanti)

Fishers look much like American martens, but are larger, with dark brown or grayish-brown fur. Notice too that fishers have no throat or chest patch. They are found in much the same areas as American martens, but are less widespread. Look for fisher tracks in old, deep woods. Fishers are active both during the day and at night. They are equally at home in trees or on the ground. They may make their den in a tree hollow or in the cleft of a rock. If you see droppings with small porcupine quills in them, they will have been made either by a fisher or a coyote.

Carnivore: Weasel family
Length: 2½–3½ ft (75–110 cm), of which tail is 12–16 in (30–41 cm)
Feeds on mice and other small rodents, porcupines, carrion, birds, fruit, and nuts
Tracks: 5 toes
Young: 1 litter of 1–5 babies

Red Squirrel
(Tamiasciurus hudsonicus)

You will probably hear a red squirrel chattering and trilling before you see it. You can recognize it from its small size and its coat, which is reddish-brown above and white below. Look for the tufts of hair on its ears and the black edging to its tail. You are most likely to see one in conifer forests in Alaska, Canada, the Rockies, or in the Appalachians. Look for discarded food piles of gnawed pine cones and acorns. It builds a nest of twigs in a treehole or on the ground. It does not hibernate in winter.

Rodent
Length: 11–15 in (28–38 cm), of which tail is 4–6 in (10–15 cm)
Feeds mainly on pine nuts and other seeds, fungi, nuts, berries, small animals, and birds' eggs
Tracks: 4 toes on front, 5 toes on back feet
Young: usually 2 litters, each with 3–7 babies

American Shrew Mole
(Neurotrichus gibbsii)

Shrew moles are the smallest moles in North America. They are found only on the West Coast from southern Canada to central California. A shrew mole looks rather like a shrew with its long, pointed nose, and its feet are not as big as those of other moles. Although it burrows, it often comes aboveground, too. You may see it walking slowly and carefully through the leaf litter (leaves on the ground) in a forest. It feeds on insects and worms it finds there.

Insectivore
Length: about 4½ in (11 cm), of which tail is 1½ in (4 cm)
Feeds on insects and salamanders
Young: more than 1 litter a year, each with 1–4 babies

Golden-mantled Ground Squirrel

(Spermophilus lateralis)

It looks much like a western chipmunk (see page 17), but it is found only in forests and on the stony slopes of the Rockies. It has no stripes across its face, but look for the two broad, white stripes on its sides. You are quite likely to see ground squirrels around camp sites. Do not try to feed these squirrels as they can be rabid and they are disease carriers. They dig a deep burrow with its entrance near a bush, rock, or log. They store food in their burrows, are active only during the day, and hibernate during the winter.

Rodent
Length: 9–12 in (23–30 cm), of which tail is 2½–4½ in (6–11 cm)
Feeds on seeds, nuts, leaves, fungi, and insects
Tracks: 4 toes on front, 5 toes on back feet
Young: 1 litter of 4–6 babies

Gapper's Red-backed Vole
(Clethrionomys gapperi)

This little animal is common across most of Canada, and extends south into the Rockies, South Dakota, New England, and North Carolina. It is smaller than a lemming and has a longer tail. You can tell it from most other voles by its reddish-brown back and gray sides. It likes forests with thick ground cover, particularly damp woods and bogs. It makes a nest under roots or logs, and stores food in the fall to see it through the winter.

Rodent
Length: 5–6 in (13–15 cm), of which tail is 1½ in (4 cm)
Feeds on green plants, shoots, seeds, berries, and fungi
Tracks: 4 toes on front, 5 toes on back feet
Young: several litters a year, each with 3–4 babies

Fox squirrels are the largest North American squirrels. Their large size is the best way to identify them. They are found all over the eastern United States except in New England. The color of their coat is usually rusty-brown above and orange below, but in Florida it is all black, in South Carolina it is black with white ears and nose, and in Maryland it is silvery gray with a white belly. Fox squirrels have been introduced into the southernmost parts of Canada and the western United States. They build their nest in a tree hole or in a hole in the ground.

Eastern Fox Squirrel
(Sciurus niger)

Rodent: Squirrel family
Length: 17–27 in (43–69 cm), of which tail is about half
Feeds on nuts, shoots, buds, berries, and fungi
Tracks: 4 toes on front, 5 toes on back feet
Young: 2 litters, each with 2–5 babies

Snowshoe Hare

(Lepus americanus)
Snowshoe hares are found throughout most of Canada, and in the United States in Alaska, the Rockies, New England, and Allegheny Mountains. In summer, their fur is rusty-brown, their short tails are white on the bottom, and their long ears are tipped with black. In winter, they are white all over except their ears, which still have black tips. Like all rabbits and hares, their feet are covered with fur. Snowshoe hares do not build nests, but lay up in shallow dips, called forms. Their young are covered with fur and can open their eyes soon after birth.

Hare and Rabbit family
Length: Up to 20 in (50 cm)
Feeds on woody shrubs, clovers, grasses, and other green plants
Tracks: 4 toes
Young: up to 4 litters, each with 2–4 babies

North American Porcupine
(Erethizon dorsatum)

The only mammal in North America to have quills, porcupines can be found in most of Canada, the western United States, and as far south as Pennsylvania in the East. They are most active at night, but you may see one lumbering through the forest or high in a tree, hunched into a large black ball. They make a den in a hollow tree or in a cave in the rocks. Listen for their grunts, groans, and high-pitched cries. Look for them along highways. A baby porcupine's quills are soft when it is born, but harden within 30 minutes. Don't go near porcupines and keep your pets away from them, as porcupines may have rabies.
Rodent—Length: 2–3 ft (60–90 cm)
Feeds on leaves, twigs, the bark of trees, and some green plants
Tracks: 5 toes with a central pad—Young: 1 baby

Signs of Mammals

Most mammals keep well out of sight of people. If you want to see them, you should keep very quiet and wear clothing that helps you blend into the landscape. Many mammals come out to feed at dusk and dawn—those are the best times to look for them. However, mammals leave lots of tracks and signs behind them that you can see at any time. Do not get too close to animals in the wild and never attempt to touch them.

What to look for

Many animals move stealthily and swiftly, but they may leave behind any of the signs shown here. Many mammals burrow deep beneath the ground or into a bank. Look for the entrance hole and paths in the grass.

footprints   half-eaten food

Map reading

The best way to pinpoint where you saw something is by giving its map reference. Maps are divided into squares by lines. Each line is lettered or numbered at the edges of the map. Suppose you spot a fox at a certain spot. You can describe this place as "on Route 66, 3 miles east of Newtown," but it is much simpler to say "Ref: 4/H."

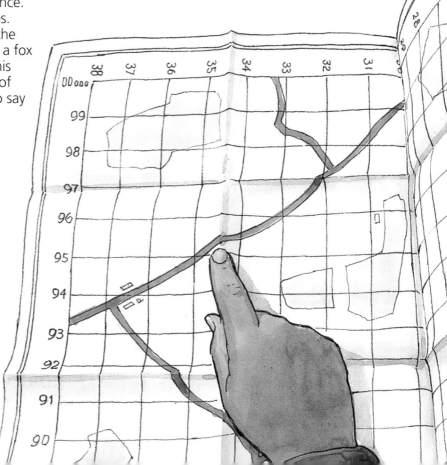

chewed bark

droppings

To give a map reference:

1 **Find the place on the map.** Ask an adult to help you if you have problems with this.
2 **Look for the first vertical (up and down) line on its left.** Follow it up or down to the edge of the map and write its letter or number in your notebook.
3 **Go back to the place on the map and find the first horizontal (across) line below it.**
4 **Follow this line to the nearest edge of the map** and write down its letter or number after the first one with a slash (/) separating the number from the letter.
5 **When you put together your final record sheets,** list all the foxes on one page, give the date when you saw each one, and the map reference. Next do the gophers, and so on.

Clothes and equipment

Your best chance of spotting mammals is when they do not know you are there. As soon as they see or hear you, they are likely to run and hide. Wear dull-colored clothes and comfortable shoes, or rubber boots. Look for mammals in quiet, secret places such as ditches, hedges, and among thick undergrowth. The best way is to sit very quietly and listen. You do not need much equipment:

1 **A lightweight backpack** to hold all your equipment.
2 **A plastic garbage bag** is useful for sitting on if the ground is wet.
3 **Pencils, pens, and a field notebook** for drawing tracks and noting what you have seen.
4 **A tape measure or ruler** to measure the size of prints and the distance between them.
5 **A pair of binoculars** may be helpful if you are looking for deer.
6 **Plastic bags** are useful for collecting specimens.
7 **Materials for making plaster casts,** if you plan on making casts of tracks (see page 49).
8 **A camera** is useful to record interesting tracks, marks on trees, dens, and so on.
9 **A flashlight** if you are watching at dusk.

You can write up your records on a separate sheet of paper for each species when you get home. Glue your sketches, drawings of tracks from your field notebook, and photographs on to the sheet as well. Keep your records in a ring binder or use a computer program.

Grasslands & Savannas

Wide, open grasslands once stretched from the Appalachians to the Rockies, covering much of North America. Most of this land is now planted with crops, and only bits of the original prairies remain.

However, you will also find prairies in California, the Southwest, and between the Rockies and the Sierra Nevada. There are two kinds of grasslands in the prairies: short grass in the West, changing to tall grass in the East. Tall grass is spectacular in spring when the wild flowers are blooming. Tall grass used to provide grazing for huge herds of bison. Short-grass prairies still stretch for many miles (or kilometers). They receive less rain than tall grass, but many small mammals such as jack rabbits, ground squirrels, and prairie dogs live there. The picture shows seven kinds of mammals from this section. How many can you recognize?

Bison (herd in distance), kit fox, black-tailed prairie dogs, pronghorns, white-tailed jack rabbit, spotted skunk, least weasel.

Kit Fox
(Vulpes velox)

Kit foxes are smaller than gray and red foxes (see page 13) and, unlike them, their fur is a grayish-yellow color all over. Look for their big ears and the black tip at the end of their tails. Kit foxes are found only in short-grass prairies and in dry, desert plains. At one time, many were killed by poisonous baits left for coyotes, and the numbers of kit foxes remains small. They hunt mainly at night, and spend most of the day in their burrows.

Carnivore: Dog family
Length: 15–20 in (38–51 cm); tail 11 in (28 cm)
Feeds on small rodents, rabbits, birds, insects, berries, and grasses
Tracks: 4 toes
Young: 1 litter of 3–6 cubs

Black-footed Ferret
(Mustela nigripes)

Black-footed ferrets look similar to the ferrets sold in pet stores. Their faces are a bit like a raccoon's with their black eye-masks, but their fur is mainly buff-colored. Look for their black feet and the black tip to their tails. They scarcely survive in the wild, and are considered to be an endangered species, because the prairie dogs (see page 37) on which they prey have been widely eliminated. Ferrets make their den under the ground.
Carnivore: Weasel family
Length: 18–22 in (46–56 cm), of which tail is a quarter
Tracks: 5 toes with central pad
Feeds on prairie dogs and other animals
Young: 1 litter of 3–5 babies

Least Weasel
(Mustela nivalis)

The least weasel is the smallest carnivore in the world. Like other weasels, it has a long, lithe body and short legs, which allow it to chase mice and voles deep into their burrows. It kills its prey by biting at the base of its skull. A least weasel is brown above and white below with a short tail. It is found throughout Canada and parts of the northern United States, but is not common anywhere. It likes grassy fields and open woods close to rivers and marshes. It is most active at night when you may hear its shrill shriek.
Carnivore: Weasel family
Length: Up to 10 in (25 cm)
Tracks: 4 toes with central pad
Feeds mostly on small mice, voles, small rabbits, birds, and other animals
Young: 2 or 3 litters, each with 3–6 young

Bison
(Bison bison)

Bison are wild oxen with large heads, necks, and shoulders. Look for the big hump of their shoulders and the long, shaggy hair on their shoulders and front legs. Huge herds of bison once roamed the plains of North America, but during the late 1800's they were almost all killed by hunters. Today, they are a protected species, and you can again see herds of bison in parks and preserves, mainly in western North America. They like to scratch themselves by rubbing their horns and heads on a boulder or tree. Look for a ring of rubbed bark about 5 feet (1.5 meters) above the ground. They also like to roll in the dust—look for bare dips in the ground where they have wallowed.

Ungulate
Length: Males, 10–12½ ft (3–3.8 m),
Females are smaller
Feeds mostly on grasses,
but also grazes on shrubs
Tracks: 2-toed, rounded hoofs
Young: 1 calf

Mustang

(Equus caballus)

Mustangs, descendants of the tame horses that were ridden by Spanish explorers, American Indians, and cowhands, look very similar to domestic ponies and horses. Look for the V-shaped mark of the mustang's hoof print to tell them apart. After having been nearly wiped out in the early 1900's, mustangs were protected in 1971, and they have become more common on the prairies since then. If you are lucky enough to be able to hide at a water hole at dawn, you may see mustangs coming to drink. Family groups usually consist of one stallion (male) and five or six mares (females). Stallions mark their territories by building up piles of droppings in selected places.

Ungulate—Length: 6½–7 ft (2–2.1 m), of which tail is 19 in (48 cm)
Feeds on grasses and shrubby plants
Tracks: a circular hoof with V-shape—Young: usually 1 foal

Pronghorn

(Antilocapra americana)

Pronghorns are the fastest animals on land in North America—they can run up to 60 mph (96 kph). Pronghorns look like antelopes, but they are not closely related to antelopes or similar animals. They are sandy-brown with a white belly and chest. The large patch of white on their rump (hind part) is the best way to tell them apart from whitetail and mule deer. When a pronghorn is alarmed, the white hairs on its rump stand up Both males and females have horns, although the females' are usually only about half the size of the males'. You will usually see pronghorns in small bands on the prairies. The males each gather about 20 females around them. When the fawns are born, they are hidden separately by the mother until they join the herd a week later.

Ungulate
Length: 4-4½ ft (1.2–1.4 m), of which tail is 2½–6½ in (6–16.5 cm)
Feeds on shrubs, and sometimes crops, such as alfalfa and wheat
Tracks: 2-toed hoofs
Young: 1–3 fawns

Spotted Skunk

(Spilogale putorius)

The spotted skunk is a small, black skunk with white stripes or spots along its head, back and sides. Its tail has a white tip. When it is alarmed, it stands on its front feet and sprays a foul-smelling scent up to a distance of 12 feet (4 meters). It will also climb trees to escape from danger, but spends most of the time on or under the ground. It is found across most of the United States. It likes open places including farmland, scrub, and woods. It hunts at night, and digs a burrow under buildings or piles of rocks. Several skunks may share a den in winter.

Carnivore: Skunk family
Length: 7–14 in (18–36 cm)
Feeds on almost anything, particularly small mammals, insects, fruit, reptiles, and carrion
Tracks: 5 toes with 4 lobes in central pad
Young: 1 litter of 4–5 babies

Hispid Cotton Rat

(Sigmodon hispidus)

Not true rats, hispid cotton rats have coarse blackish or dark grizzled-brown fur, with whitish bellies. Their ears are almost hidden by their fur, and their tails are fairly short and scaly. They are found in grassy fields in the southeastern United States. Look for the runways they make through the grass. They leave small piles of cut grass stems along them. They make a nest on the surface or in a burrow. The young leave the nest before they are a week old, and can breed when they are only six weeks old. Cotton rats seldom live for more than a year, but they can cause a lot of damage to sugarcane, sweet potatoes, and other crops.

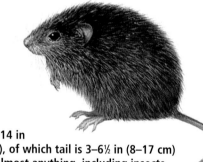

Rodent
Length: 8–14 in
(20–36 cm), of which tail is 3–6½ in (8–17 cm)
Feeds on almost anything, including insects, crabs, birds and their eggs, and crops
Tracks: 4 toes on front, 5 toes on back feet
Young: several litters, each of 2–12 babies

Meadow Jumping Mouse

Rodent
Length: 7–10 in (18–25 cm), of which tail is more than half
Feeds on seeds, grasses, fungi, beetles, and other insects
Tracks: 4 toes on front, 5 toes on back feet
Young: 2 or 3 litters, each with 2–8 babies

(Zapus hudsonius)
This small mouse is darker above than below, and has long hind legs. When it is startled, it makes a few bounding jumps and then freezes. If you see it do this, you could possibly mistake it for a frog. This mouse is found in meadows, marshes, and the edge of forests across most of Canada, and south into the United States to Oklahoma and Georgia. It is most active at night, and builds a nest below the ground in which it hibernates for up to eight months in winter. In April or May, it emerges and builds a nest on the surface of the ground or beneath a log or tree stump.

Black-tailed Prairie Dog
(Cynomys ludovicianus)

These prairie dogs are bigger than most other ground squirrels, but are slightly smaller than a cat. Their fur is pale brown above and whitish below. If you can get close enough to one, look at its tail to see if it has a black or white tip. Only the black-tailed prairie dog has a black tip to its tail. Look for bare mounds of earth 10–20 yards (9–18 meters) apart and about 1–2 feet (30–60 centimeters) high. This is a sign that there is a prairie dog town under the ground. One animal keeps watch on a mound of earth while the rest of the group feeds. If the look-out spots danger it barks to alert the town. Many prairie dogs have been killed and their habitats destroyed to create grazing land for sheep and cows, and so their population has been greatly reduced.

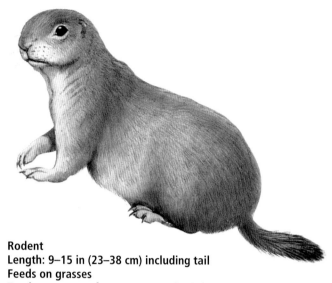

Rodent
Length: 9–15 in (23–38 cm) including tail
Feeds on grasses
Tracks: 4 toes on front, 5 toes on back feet
Young: 1 litter of 1–6 babies

Thirteen-lined Ground Squirrel

(Spermophilus tridecemlineatus)
This ground squirrel gets its name from the 13 dark brown and creamy-buff stripes down its back. Notice how the lighter stripes are often broken into spots. Unlike chipmunks (page 17), it has no stripes on its face. It lives alone, and likes shortgrass prairies. If you live in central states, you may also come across one on a golf course, beside the road, or even in your own backyard. Listen for its sharp alarm call, followed by a musical chattering when it is safely back in its shallow burrow. It hibernates between October and March.

Rodent
Length: 6½–11½ in (17–29 cm), of which tail is 2½–5 in (5–13 cm)
Feeds on almost anything, particularly insects, grass, and other plants
Tracks: 4 toes on front, 5 toes on back feet
Young: 1 litter of 8–10 babies

Richardson's Ground Squirrel
(Spermophilus richardsoni)

Richardson's ground squirrel is one of the most common mammals on the shortgrass prairies and sagebrush scrub. Its fur is smoky-gray mixed with buff. Its long tail is edged with white or buff. Like most other ground squirrels, it digs burrows in the ground and lives close to other members of its species in loose colonies. Watch for one standing on its back legs, looking out for intruders. And listen for its warning whistle which sends all the others fleeing back to their burrows. Richardson's ground squirrels store food in their burrows. The adults estivate (sleep through the hottest summer months) until September, and hibernate through the coldest winter months. Like other ground squirrels they are known to carry plague.

Rodent
Length: 10–14 in (25–36 cm), of which tail is 2½–4½ in (6–11 cm)
Feeds mostly on grass, roots, and other plants, including crops
Tracks: 4 toes on front, 5 toes on back feet
Young: usually 1 litter of 6–11 babies

White-tailed Jack Rabbit
(Lepus townsendi)

Rabbit and Hare family
Length: 22–25 in (56–63 cm), of which tail is 2½–4 in (6–10 cm)
Feeds on plants with thick, juicy leaves or stems
Tracks: 4 toes; back prints are much longer than front ones
Young: 1 or 2 litters, each with 3–6 babies

The white-tailed jack rabbit is a hare. Like other hares and rabbits, it has long ears and a short tail. Its fur is grayish-brown in summer, but pale gray in winter. The best way to tell it from other jack rabbits is to look at its tail, which is white both above and below. White-tailed jack rabbits are found in open plains and pastures mainly in the United States from California to Iowa. They have long hind legs, and you may see them fleeing at high speed through the grass. If they are chased, they will run in a huge circle, a mile (or about a kilometer) or more across. They can also jump a gap of up to 17 feet (4.3 meters). They forage for food at night and, unless disturbed, sit in their lairs during the day. They do not burrow into the ground, but they make tunnels in deep snow.

Western Pocket Gophers
(Thomomys)

A western pocket gopher has a large, blunt head and short legs. It has fur-lined pouches in each cheek which it packs with food to take back to its tunnel. The claws on the front feet are long and curved and are very useful for digging burrows. You can tell if there are gophers about because they push fan-shaped mounds of earth up to the surface as they burrow. Western pocket gophers live on their own for most of their lives and are active during the day and at night. They are seldom seen aboveground, but will sometimes come to the surface to forage for plants, which they bite off below ground level and then drag into their tunnels. Although they may damage crops, they probably do more good to the soil than harm. Different species of western pocket gophers live in different regions in the western United States.

Rodent
Length: 7–10½ in (18–27 cm), of which tail is 2–3½ in (5–9 cm)
Feeds on plants, bulbs, and roots
Tracks: 4 toes on front, 5 toes on back feet
Young: 1 or 2 litters, each with 2–10 babies

Southeastern pocket gopher
(Geomys pinetis)

Plains pocket gopher
(Geomys bursarius)

Eastern Pocket Gophers
(Geomys)

The only difference between eastern pocket gophers and western pocket gophers is that the first have grooves down the center of their teeth, but you are hardly likely to see those. Like the western pocket gopher, the color of their fur varies from one region to another. Notice their small eyes and ears, surrounded by short, thick fur, and the long claws on their front feet. They like loose, sandy soils best in which to dig their burrows. In winter, they tunnel through snow, and push loose dirt from the ground underneath into these tunnels. When the snow melts, look for the long "ropes" of dirt that remain on the surface of the ground.

Rodent
Length: 7–14 in (18–36 cm), of which tail is 2–4½ in (5–11 cm)
Feeds on plants, particularly roots and bulbs
Tracks: 4 toes on front, 5 toes on back feet
Young: several litters, each with 1–8 babies

Southern Bog Lemming
(Synaptomys cooperi)

This small lemming looks much like a field vole (see page 41), but its tail is even shorter, and its fur is more brownish than grayish. It is found in much of eastern North America from Quebec to North Carolina. In spite of its name, it likes grassy meadows, not bogs or marshes. It is active during the day and at night. Like field voles, it makes runways through the grass, and leaves piles of cut grass stems along them where it has been feeding. Look for its bright green droppings. It may build its nest of grass above the ground or in a burrow.

Rodent
Length: 4½–6 in (11–15 cm), of which tail is ½–1 in (1–2.5 cm)
Feeds on leaves, grass seed, moss, fungi, and some insects
Tracks: 4 toes on front, 5 toes on back feet spread wide
Young: several litters, each with 3–5 babies

Nine-banded Armadillo
(Dasypus novemcinctus)

It is easy to recognize a nine-banded armadillo. It is the only mammal in North America to have a hard, "armored" shell. It can curl up inside its shell when it is threatened, but it usually dashes for safety into its burrow or thick bushes. Notice that the top of its head and its tail are protected as well as its body. Armadillos were once found only in South America and the extreme southeastern United States. They have spread northward, however, and are now found in crop fields from South Carolina to Oklahoma. You are most likely to see an armadillo early in the morning or in the evening. Watch it snuffling in the leaf mold for food. You may also see it rolling in mud at a water hole or by a stream.

Xenarthran
Length: 2 ft (61 cm) including tail
Feeds on insects, spiders, land snails, earthworms, and eggs
Tracks: 4 toes on front feet, 5 toes on back feet
Young: 1 litter of 4 babies of the same sex

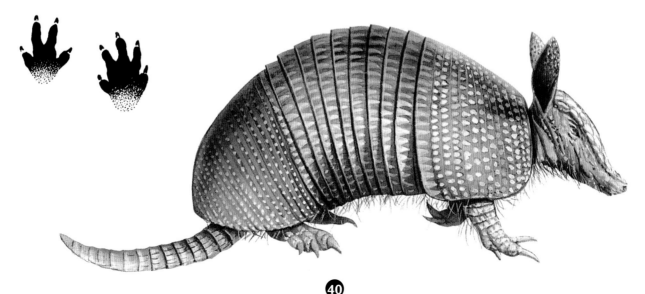

Harvest Mouse

Rodent
Length: 4–7½ in (10–18 cm), of which tail is nearly half
Feeds mostly on seeds and plants
Tracks: 4 toes on front, 5 toes on back feet
Young: several litters, each with 1–7 babies

(Micromys minutus)
Harvest mice look much like house mice (see page 19). Their fur is usually brownish above and white below, and they have big ears and eyes, and long tails. Unlike house mice, harvest mice have a groove down their upper teeth. Harvest mice climb well, but are hard to spot among the vegetation. Look instead for their round nest of grasses. They may build them on the ground, or aboveground, in vines, bushes, and woodpecker holes. They breed throughout the year except in the north, where they breed in the warm months.

Northern Short-tailed Shrew

(Blarina brevicauda)

You can tell this is a shrew by its long, pointed nose, small eyes, and soft, velvety fur. As its name implies, its tail is shorter than most other shrews. Its saliva (spit) is poisonous, and one bite is usually enough to paralyze its prey. They are found in woods, swamps, and bogs, as well as in grasslands, over the eastern United States and north into eastern Canada. They are very busy animals and are active during the day as well as at night, hunting for food and tunneling in the ground or under the snow. They also use tunnels and runways made by mice and other small rodents.
Insectivore
Length: 3½–5 in (9–13 cm), of which tail is about 1 in (2.5 cm)
Feeds on insects, worms, snails, and young mice
Tracks: 5 toes
Young: up to 3 litters, each with 3–7 babies

Field Vole

(Microtus agrestis)

You can tell voles or lemmings from mice and rats because voles and lemmings have small ears and eyes, and shorter tails. Field voles, also called meadow voles, have grayish fur and are found in grassy areas all over Canada and in most of the United States. Look in long grass for signs of them—they make little paths radiating out through the grass from their burrow. Look for piles of cut grass stems along their runways. In winter, look for field voles' tooth marks on the bark of bushes. Like gophers (see page 39), they tunnel through the snow in winter, filling the tunnels with grass, dirt, and sticks, which are revealed when the snow melts. In summer, they dig burrows under the ground, although some build their round nest in plants overhanging a stream and swim to and from the nest. Weasels prey on voles, and may take over voles' nests and line them with their victims' fur.
Rodent
Length: 5½–8 in (14–20 cm), of which tail is 1–2½ in (2.5–6 cm)
Feeds on plants, particularly grass, twigs, roots, and bulbs
Tracks: 4 toes on front feet, 5 toes on back feet spread wide
Young: several litters, each with up to 9 babies

Hunting for Hunters

Many carnivores (meat-eaters) hunt at night and live alone. These animals are often difficult to see. Look for their dens and burrows instead, as well as their tracks and droppings, bits of fur, and other signs they often leave behind them.

River Otters
(Lutra canadensis)

Look for signs of river otters along lakesides and riverbanks in wooded country. Otters are playful creatures—sometimes they make a slide down a muddy bank straight into the water. They regularly leave their droppings in very obvious places, on logs and large stones, often near the entrance to their den. Otter droppings are called "spraints." They are very soft and dark green when fresh, with a strong, musky smell. As they dry, they turn white and look like piles of cigar ash. If you break one open with a twig, you may see fish scales and bones in them. (Wash your hands after you have done this.)

Badger's sett

If you see a mound of earth in front of the entrance to a large den, it probably belongs to a badger. The burrow of a badger is called a sett. Look around the entrance for other signs. Badgers are very clean animals. They use a special place or hollow as a latrine for their droppings.

Look for dry grass, leaves, and other bedding materials which the badger has dropped as it takes them to its den. Examine nearby trees for scratch marks where the badger has cleaned its claws. It also rubs its fur on the bark. Can you find any hairs or dirt sticking to the bark?

Caught on the wire

As animals crawl through barbed wire, some of their hair may get caught in it. You will easily find sheep's wool in spiky bushes and barbed wire, but look for the fur of rabbits and badgers as well.

Whose hole in the ground?

Foxes, badgers, and other carnivores dig dens into the ground or under thick bushes. The size of the hole is a good clue to its maker. Fox and badger holes are about 1 foot (30 centimeters) wide. Rabbit holes are about 4 inches (10 centimeters) wide. Vole and mouse holes are about 2 inches (5 centimeters) wide.

Tracks

Foxes and cats both leave paw prints with four toes, rather like those of a dog. To tell them apart, notice how the toes are arranged around the central pad. Many members of the weasel family, including skunks and badgers, leave five-toed prints. If the tracks are clear, you can often tell more from them than simply which animal has made them.

- Can you tell tracks made by the front feet from those of the back feet?
- How far apart are they?
- Do you think the animal was walking or running?
- Is there more than one set of prints? If so, was one animal chasing the other?
- Look to see if there is the mark of a long tail dragging on the ground.

Deserts

In a desert, the ground is very dry and there is little plant life. It may rain from time to time, but never for long. Desert animals have to survive for most of the year without rain water.

Most desert plants survive the dry conditions by storing water in their stems or in bulbs under the ground. Many cacti are protected by sharp spines, but peccaries, for example, eat the juicy fruits of prickly pears. Other mammals dig up bulbs, while rodents get enough water from the seeds and grains they eat.

Much of the American desert is very hot during the day. Most mammals there feed at night. During the day they hide in rock crevices or underground. Bats roost in caves and feed on insects or nectar from cactus flowers. The picture shows five kinds of mammals from this book. How many can you identify?

Spotted bat, northern grasshopper mouse, collared peccaries, ringtail, desert shrew.

Little Long-nosed Bat

(Leptonycteris yerbabuenae)

The little long-nosed bat is found only in the extreme south of Arizona and New Mexico, and only in the summer. It has a long nose and a stunted tail. If you see one close-up, look for the leaflike flap of skin at the end of its nose. It comes to the United States from Mexico to mate and give birth—colonies of several thousand mothers gather with their babies in caves, mines, and tunnels. While the mothers go out to collect pollen from agave, saguaro, and organ pipe cacti, the babies are left hanging on their own.

Bat
Length: about 3 in (8 cm)
Feeds on nectar and pollen of cacti
Young: 1–2 babies

Peters' Ghost-faced Bat

(Mormoops megalophylla)

If you get the chance to look closely at this bat, you will see that it has leaflike folds of skin across its chin. They stretch to its ears and are not found on any other North American bat. Its fur is brown. It is a strong flier, and you may see it in the deserts of Arizona, Texas, and Mexico. It likes to roost in caves and old mines, and particularly likes hot, humid sites. Although only a few roosting sites are known in Texas, some of them have several thousand bats in them. Farther south, in Mexico, roosts have been found with up to half a million bats.

Bat
Length: about 2½ in (6 cm)
Feeds on insects, particularly moths
Young: 1 baby

Spotted Bat

(Euderma maculatum)

Spotted bats are quite spectacular. They have huge, pink ears and three large, white spots on their dark brown backs. They have occasionally been found as far north as British Columbia and Montana but are more common in the desert farther south. You will be very lucky to see one—it is one of the rarest bats in North America.

Bat
Length: 4 in (10 cm), of which tail is 2 in (5 cm)
Feeds on insects
Young: 1 baby

Northern Grasshopper Mouse
(Onychomys leucogaster)

A northern grasshopper mouse is stouter than most other mice, and has a shorter tail. Its fur is grayish- or pinkish-cinnamon, and the tip of its tail is white. The northern grasshopper mouse is found in dry prairies as well as in the desert, and it is most active at night. You might hear it—it stands on its back legs and it calls out in a loud, high-pitched howl. It usually lives in the burrow once inhabited by a ground squirrel, prairie dog, or pocket gopher.

Rodent
**Length: 5–7½ in
(13–19 cm),
of which tail is
1–2 in
(2.5–5 cm)**

Feeds mostly on grasshoppers and other insects, small mice, scorpions, and some plants
Tracks: 4 toes on front, 5 toes on hind feet
Young: 2–3 litters, each with 2-6 babies

Insectivore
Length: 3–3½ in (8-9 cm), of which tail is about 1 in (2.5 cm)
Feeds on insects
Tracks: 5 toes
Young: 2 litters, each with up to 6 babies

Desert Shrew
(Notiosorex crawfordi)

Desert shrews have long noses and small, beady eyes. Their fur is gray, and their ears are larger than those of other shrews. They are found in the southwestern United States and in Mexico. Look for them around sagebrush and prickly pears, or in garbage dumps where they hunt for food. Look for their nests beneath agave plants or under boards or debris. Their nests are made with fine plant stems and sometimes with hair.

Pygmy Rabbit
(Brachylagus idahoensis)

Pygmy rabbits are the smallest rabbits in North America, and the only ones to dig a burrow. You can tell them from similar-looking animals by their size. They are smaller than eastern cottontail rabbits (see page 18), and larger than pikas (see page 54). They do not have a white tail like cottontails, but they do have a rabbit's long ears. Look for them where there is plenty of sagebrush, and also in sand dunes. Although they are most active at night, you may see them during the day. Their simple burrow has three or more entrances.

Rabbit and hare family
Length: 10–11 in (25–28 cm), of which tail is less than 1 in (2.5 cm)
Feeds mainly on sagebrush
Tracks: 4 toes surrounded by foot
Young: 1 litter of 5–8 babies

White-tailed Antelope-squirrel

(Ammospermophilus leucurus)

With its buff-colored fur, a white-tailed antelope squirrel is well camouflaged in the desert, except that it usually runs with its tail held tightly over its back, allowing the tail's white underside to flash in the sun. It looks similar to a chipmunk (see page 17), but is paler and a chipmunk does not have a white undertail. Antelope squirrels do not need to drink because they get all the moisture they need from their food. They can be seen among rock crevices or peeking out of their burrows all day. They bounce as they move. The young are born underground in a nest lined with feathers, fur, and plant fibers.

Rodent
Length: 7½–9 in (19–23 cm), of which tail is 2–3 in (5–8 cm)
Feeds on the seeds of cacti, yucca, and other desert plants, and on insects
Tracks: 4 toes on front, 5 toes on hind feet
Young: 1 litter of 5–14 babies

Antelope Jack Rabbit

(Lepus alleni)

Antelope jack rabbits are large hares with long legs and ears up to 7½ inches (19 centimeters) long. You are most likely to notice their white undertail flashing through the cacti as they bound away. They are active from early in the evening until after dawn. During the day they rest in the shade of a bush, then groups of 20 or more move off to feed. They do not dig burrows, but the mother makes a nest in the ground or in a hollow cactus and lines it with fur. Sometimes, she leaves each baby in a separate hiding place.

Rabbit and hare family
Length: 21–26 in (53–66 cm), of which tail is 2–3 in (5–8 cm)
Feeds on grasses, mesquite, cacti, and other desert plants
Tracks: 4 toes surrounded by feet, which are much longer
Young: up to 7 litters, each with 1–5 babies

Collared Peccary

(Tayassu tajacu)

You can recognize a collared peccary by its snout and piglike shape. Its fur is coarse and grizzled gray or black. Look for the collar of paler fur around its neck. You are most likely to see peccaries in bands of several hundred animals in the morning or late afternoon. Look for them in chaparral, rocky canyons, and among scrub oaks as well as in the desert. The young have reddish fur with a black stripe down their backs. They are able to follow their mother only a few days after birth.

Ungulate: Peccary family—Length: 3 ft (91 cm), of which tail is 2 in (5 cm)
Feeds on cacti, prickly pears, and other desert plants
Tracks: 2-toed hoofs—Young: up to 5 babies (usually 2)

Tracking Deer

Deer are often easy to spot. There are many herds in national parks, and you can often get quite close to them without them running off. Be careful in the fall, however, when they are rutting (or mating) because they can be very bad tempered then.

You may also see deer in forests or on mountains, as well as bighorn sheep and mountain goats. Watch for them on the skyline. Look for their tracks, droppings, and other signs that they are nearby.

Discarded antlers

Most male deer grow antlers and shed them once each year. Four to six months later they have grown a new pair. Even in places where there are lots of deer you will be lucky to find a shed antler. They usually disappear because mice and other small mammals eat them up. You can sometimes tell how old a male deer is from the size of his antlers and the number of points they have.

While a deer's new antlers are growing they are covered by a furry skin called "velvet." It contains blood vessels that help the antlers grow. When the antlers are fully grown, the blood dries up and the deer rubs the velvet off on low branches, leaving shiny, bony antlers.

Signs left on trees

Deer will strip bark off trees to eat, as well as use the trunk to remove the velvet from their antlers. How high they strip the tree depends on the deer. Moose can strip bark up to 10 feet (3 meters) high and elk up to 6 feet (1.8 meters), but mule deer do not go much higher than 3 feet (91 centimeters). Bighorn sheep also bite into bark. Look for the tooth marks to tell them apart. Deer leave deep, vertical marks, while sheep make slanting marks. Squirrels and small mammals leave much smaller tooth marks.

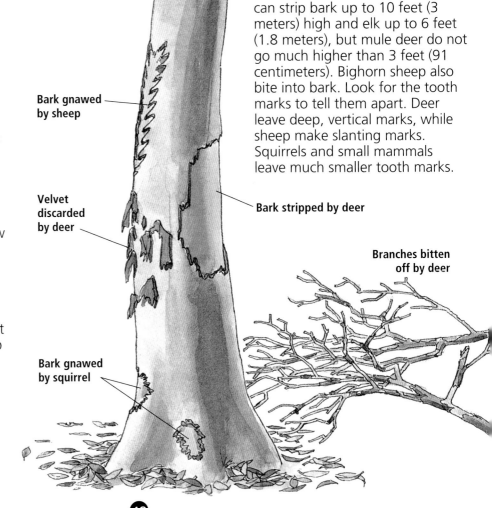

Bark gnawed by sheep

Velvet discarded by deer

Bark gnawed by squirrel

Bark stripped by deer

Branches bitten off by deer

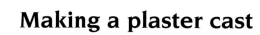

Making a plaster cast

1. **Bend a strip of stiff cardboard into a ring** a bit bigger than the footprint and fasten it with a paper clip.
2. **Clear away any leaves or twigs** from the print and push the cardboard into the ground so that the print is in the middle.
3. **Half fill a yogurt cup** with plaster of Paris and mix with water to make a thick paste.
4. **Pour the paste into the ring** all over the print and leave to set for about 30 minutes.
5. **Slide a knife under the cast** and lift it gently.
6. **Remove the cardboard and clean** the mud off the cast, after it is thoroughly dry, with a nailbrush and water.

Footprints in the mud

If you find some clear prints in soft mud or snow, draw them in your notebook. If the prints have cloven hoofs, you will know they were made by a deer, cow, goat, or sheep.

Droppings

Whatever the weather, animals always leave droppings, and they are one of the best ways of telling which animals are around. Look at the size, shape, and color to tell them apart, but do not touch them. Meat-eaters' droppings are usually long and contain undigested bits of animals. Plant-eaters' droppings are usually round or oval and contain plant fibers.

Mouse

Rabbit

Weasel

Fox

Deer

Sheep

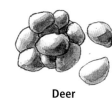

Badger

Mountains & Tundras

The Rocky Mountains are the largest mountain system in North America. West of the Rockies are the Sierra Nevada and the Cascade Range. In the East are the Appalachian Mountains. In the far north, a region called the tundra lies between the Arctic snows and the coniferous forests. Living on the tundra is very similar to mountain living.

In winter, mountains and tundra are covered with a thick blanket of snow for several months. Icy winds sweep across the ground so that only a few small, hardy plants can survive there. Many animals migrate to avoid the harshest weather. Caribou move south into the forests, while some mountain sheep and goats move lower down the slopes. Smaller mammals, such as marmots, hibernate in the winter or live under the snow.

The climate is so harsh that the number of some mammals varies considerably from year to year. In very cold winters many animals, particularly small rodents, die. The animals that feed on them are affected, too. Arctic foxes prey on lemmings and other rodents, so when there are fewer lemmings, there are fewer foxes, too.

Most of the mammals have thick fur to protect them from the cold. Unfortunately, they have been much hunted for their beautiful fur. Some are now rare and in danger of extinction. The picture shows eight kinds of mammals from this book. How many can you recognize?

Grizzly bear, woodland caribou (herd in distance), moose, Arctic fox, mountain goat, hoary marmot, musk oxen, gray wolves.

Mountains & Tundras

Hog-nosed Skunk
(Conepatus mesoleucus)

You can tell this is a skunk from its black-and-white fur and bushy tail. Unlike other skunks, its back and tail are completely white. It gets the name "hog-nosed" from its bare, piglike snout and, like pigs, it uses this snout to root in the ground for much of its food. This skunk is most active at night, and during the day, you can look for patches of ground it has "plowed" up in search of grubs. It lives mostly in the foothills of the southwestern United States. It likes partly wooded and rocky areas far away from humans. It lives on its own and makes a den in a cleft in the rocks. Like other skunks, it defends itself by spraying a foul scent at its attacker.

Carnivore: Weasel family
Length: 14–19 in (36–48 cm)
Feeds on insects, reptiles, spiders, plants, and small mammals
Tracks: 5 toes with pad
Young: 1 litter of 3–4 babies

Ringtail
(Bassariscus astutus)

A ringtail looks a bit like a cat with its large ears and big eyes. Its fur is tan to grayish-tan above and buff below. You cannot miss its long tail with black-and white rings. Raccoons have similar tails, but they are much larger and have black-and-white face markings. Ringtails are secretive animals—they are most active at night and keep out of sight. They like dry, rocky places with cliffs and canyons, or woody places near water. They do not often leave tracks. They make their den in caves, rock crevices, and hollow trees. When ringtails are cornered, they release a foul smell from a gland under their tail.

Carnivore: Ringtail family
Length: 25–32 in (64–81 cm) including tail of 12–17 in (30–43 cm)
Feeds on small mammals, crickets, grasshoppers, scorpions, reptiles, fruit, and berries
Tracks: 5 toes
Young: 1 litter of 2–4 babies

Wolverine

Carnivore: Weasel family
Length: 3½ ft (110 cm)
Feeds on berries, shoots, and any animal it can catch
Tracks: 5-toed paw prints—Young: a litter of 2–5 babies

(Gulo gulo)

This animal is the largest member of the weasel family, and it looks like a small bear. Its shaggy coat is very dark brown with paler patches across its forehead and down its sides. It has large feet and thick legs. Wolverines live mainly in the Arctic, and they are found across Alaska and northern Canada and south into the Rockies. They live on their own and are active day and night. They may travel many miles (or kilometers) scavenging for food, and wolverines can smell carrion (dead animals) even under several feet (or meters) of snow. They rob traps and are known to steal from trappers' food stores. Their powerful jaws can crunch through the bones of large animals such as moose. Wolverines do not make a permanent burrow, but use any sheltered place they find.

American Black Bear
(Ursus americanus)

Bears are large carnivores (meat-eaters) but they will eat almost anything they can find. They have small, rounded ears, and their short tail is hidden in their thick fur. American black bears are found over most of Canada, south into the Rockies to Mexico, and along the East Coast to Florida. Black bears who live in the East have blackish fur. In the West, they are often a cinnamon-brown and may be confused with a grizzly bear (see right). They live on their own and hunt mainly at night, but they leave plenty of signs behind them. Look for mammal burrows that have been dug up, or strips of bark bitten or pulled off pine, spruce, or fir trees. Young black bears sometimes climb aspen trees, leaving their claw marks in the bark. Bears also like to rub themselves against a favorite tree—look for bits of hair stuck to the bark. Black bears sleep in their dens made in a hollow tree or beneath roots.

Carnivore: Bear family
Length: 5 ft (1.5 m)
Feeds on almost everything, including insects, small mammals, berries, leaves, carrion, fish, and honey
Tracks: 5 toes with pad
Young: 1 litter of 1–4 cubs

Grizzly Bear
(Ursus arctos)

The grizzly is a brown bear that gets its name from the white tips to its brownish or yellowish fur. Grizzlies can be easily annoyed and can be very dangerous if threatened, particularly when they are with their cubs. They live in the wild mainly in Alaska and western Canada, but are still found in the Rockies as far south as Yellowstone National Park. If you are camping in the park, keep your food outside your tent, so if a grizzly comes to raid it, you will not meet it face to face! If you are in bear country, it is important to be able to recognize any signs that grizzlies are about. Look for their droppings and tracks, for bark ripped off trees, and for bear hairs stuck to bark. Grizzly bears live on their own, and make a den in a cave or among tree roots. They hunt mostly at dawn and dusk, but you may come across one at other times, too. They hide uneaten carcasses, sometimes by lying on top of them for two to three weeks. If you find a carcass, get away from it. A grizzly may not be far away and will attack to defend its food supply.

Carnivore: Bear family
Length: up to 8 ft (2.4 m)
Feeds on small animals, fruit, grubs, fish, and anything it can find
Tracks: 5 toes
Young: 1 litter of 1–4 cubs, every second year

Mountains & Tundras

American Pika
(*Ochotona princeps*)

Pikas look much like guinea pigs, but have larger, furry ears. They are also called conies, little chief hares, or calling hares. They live in large colonies among piles of rock fragments, high in the mountains from British Columbia south to California and New Mexico. Listen for their loud, squeaking calls. They collect plants and leave them to dry among the rocks before taking them underground to their dens. If you see a stack of plants and grasses, look among the rocks around you. You may well see a pika hunched up and camouflaged on a boulder. Watch it hop to its den deep among the rocks. Look too for its black, sticky droppings.

Pika family
Length: 7 in (18 cm)
Feeds on a wide range of plants
Tracks: 4 toes surrounded by foot
Young: 1–2 litters, each with 2–6 babies

Nuttall's Cottontail
(*Sylvilagus nuttalli*)

Rabbit and hare family
Length: 13–16 in (33–41 cm), of which tail is 1½–2 in (4–5 cm)
Feeds on grasses, sagebrush, juniper, and other woody shrubs
Tracks: 4 toes surrounded by foot
Young: 3–5 litters, each with 3–8 babies

This is the cottontail you are most likely to see in the Rockies from the Canadian border south to New Mexico. It is also known as the mountain cottontail. It is grayish-brown above and white below. Look for its large, grizzled tail. Its ears are shorter than those of many other rabbits. It feeds mostly in the early evening and during the morning. During the day, it lays up in a hollow in the ground, among the rocks, or in an underground burrow.

Sagebrush Vole
(*Lemmiscus curtatus*)

Rodent
Length: 4½–5½ in (11–14 cm), of which tail is ½–1 in (1–2.5 cm)
Feeds on the leaves and woody parts of sagebrush
Tracks: 4 toes on front, 5 toes on hind feet
Young: usually more than 1 litter, each with 3–6 babies

Look for this small vole among sagebrush steppes and dry prairies in the Rockies from Washington south to eastern California. It is pale gray above and whitish below, and is the only vole you are likely to see here. It is active day and night and builds its nest under shrubs. Look for the shallow tunnels it makes from its nest to nearby shrubs. Sagebrush voles live in loose colonies, so if you see one animal, look around for signs of others, too.

Eastern Woodrat

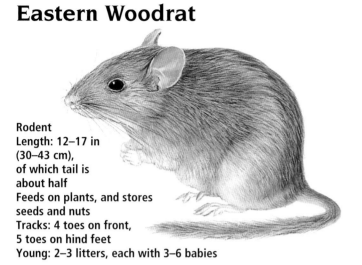

Rodent
Length: 12–17 in
(30–43 cm),
of which tail is
about half
Feeds on plants, and stores
seeds and nuts
Tracks: 4 toes on front,
5 toes on hind feet
Young: 2–3 litters, each with 3–6 babies

(Neotoma floridana)
Eastern woodrats look like brown rats (see page 14), but their tails are furry and their ears are larger. They are gray-brown above and white below, and are found in most of the eastern United States, but not north of Pennsylvania. They are most active at night, so you will be lucky to see these animals, but you will certainly see their houses. Look for large piles of twigs, sticks, and leaves decorated with bottle tops, gun shells, and other bright objects. (On the plains they build houses up to 4 feet [1–2 meters] across and almost as high.) They build their houses over their nests, which may be dug underground or made in a crack of a rock or in a hollow tree. You will notice the distinctive smell of their dens.

Hoary Marmot
(Marmota caligata)

Hoary marmots are usually found higher up in the mountains and farther north than yellow-bellied marmots. They are sometimes called mountain marmots. Their fur is mostly silvery-gray. Look for their black-and-white faces among the stones of a rockslide and for the large mounds of dirt, which show where their burrows are. Listen for their shrill warning whistle. They feed during the day, but hibernate from October to February.

Rodent
Length: 17–32 in (43–81 cm), of which tail is
6½–9½ in (17–24 cm)
Feeds mostly on grass and green leaves
Tracks: 4 toes on front, 5 toes on hind feet
Young: 1 litter of 4–5 babies

Yellow-bellied Marmot
(Marmota flaviventris)

The yellow-bellied marmot is yellowish-brown above and, as its name implies, has a yellowish belly. It has a heavy body and a longish tail. You may see it on rocky hillsides of the Rockies, the Cascades, and the Sierras. It feeds during the day, and makes its den among rock piles or in a burrow. The entrance to the den is usually near a large boulder, which it uses as a lookout post. Listen for its high-pitched chirp, which warns other marmots of danger.

Rodent—Length: 18–27 in (46–69 cm), of which tail is
5–8½ in (13–22 cm)
Feeds on green plants, such as grasses and lupines
Tracks: 4 toes on front, 5 toes on hind feet
Young: 1 litter of about 5 babies

Mountains & Tundras

American Elk
(Cervus elaphus)

At one time, elk roamed over much of North America, but now there are only a scattered few outside the Rockies. They are reddish-brown with a yellowish rump and tail. You are most likely to see elk in a forest in a group of 25 or more animals. You can easily tell the bulls (males) from the cows (females). Bulls are larger and have shaggy hair around their neck. In later summer and fall, they have large, branching antlers. Cows do not have antlers. Listen for the bull's buglelike call, as he defends his group of females from other males. Males shed their antlers in February or March, and the elk move higher up the mountains in spring.

Ungulate
Length: 6½–9½ ft (2–2.9 meters), of which tail is 3–8½ in (8–22 cm)
Feeds on grasses and shrubs
Tracks: 2-toed hoofs
Young: usually a single calf, sometimes twins

Mountain Goat
(Oreamnos americanus)

You cannot mistake a mountain goat, with its shaggy white fur, white beard, and black eyes, nose, horns, and hoofs, but you will have to climb high up the mountains to see it. Look for it on rocky crags near the snowline. It is found in the Rockies from Alaska south to Montana and Idaho, and has been introduced into nearby states as well. Unlike deer, mountain goats have horns that never branch and are never shed. Both males and females have them. A mountain goat is a superb climber and often makes its bed on a rocky ledge. Its droppings look like those of deer or sheep.

Ungulate
Length: 4–5½ ft (1.2–1.7 m), of which tail is 3–8 in (8–20 cm)
Feeds on grasses, shrubs, and other plants
Tracks: 2-toed hoofs
Young: 1 kid

Bighorn Sheep
(Ovis canadensis)

You may see bighorn sheep not only in the foothills and on the meadows of the mountains, but also in the prairies and deserts from Alberta to northwestern Mexico. They are usually brown above and paler below, although in the desert they are pale all over. The rams (males) have huge, coiled horns. The ewes (females) are smaller than the rams and their horns do not coil. In the winter, bighorns live together in herds of up to 100 animals. Males and females usually live apart in smaller groups of about 10 in summer. During the mating season, the males compete with each other for females, and then you can hear their horns clashing up to a mile (or kilometer) away. Look for their "beds" on rocky outposts—they scrape the ground to make a shallow dip, then lie down. A bighorn sheep will return to the same bed again and again, so there is always a lot of dung nearby.

Ungulate
Length: 5–6 ft (1.5–2.0 m), of which tail is 3–5 in (8–13 cm)
Feeds on grasses, sedges, shrubs, and other plants, including cacti
Tracks: 2-toed hoofs
Young: 1 lamb, sometimes twins

Barbary Sheep
(Ammotragus lervia)

Barbary sheep, also known as aoudads, have been introduced into North America from North Africa and are now probably more common here than in Africa. They are tawny-brown and have a long beard. Notice how their horns bend outward. You can see them in dry canyons and on rocky hillsides in the southwestern United States and Mexico. They do not need to drink water because they get enough moisture from dew and the plants they eat.

Ungulate
Length: 4–6 ft (1.2–2.0 m), of which tail is 9½ in (24 cm)
Feeds on grasses, shrubs, and crops
Tracks: 2-toed hoofs
Young: 1–3 lambs

Arctic Fox
(Alopex lagopus)

Arctic foxes vary in color: in summer, they are brown or grayish-white, while in winter they are white or slate-blue. Arctic foxes are slightly smaller than red foxes (see page 13) and have smaller ears and bushier tails. They live in Alaska and northern Canada, and their feet are heavily covered with fur to protect them from the cold. They are not shy of humans and come close to the homes of people. They follow polar bears in winter, hoping to feed on the carrion they leave behind. They use established dens and do not roam far from there until the cubs are old enough to take care of themselves. They are usually silent, although they can bark, howl, yelp, and wail. The warning cries of birds are the most likely sign that an Arctic fox is about.

Carnivore: Dog family
Length: 20 in (50 cm) excluding tail
Feeds mainly on lemmings, nesting birds, and carrion left by polar bears and wolves
Tracks: 4-toed paw prints
Young: 1 litter, usually of 5–10 cubs

Polar Bear
(Ursus maritimus)

You cannot mistake a polar bear—if you see one in a zoo, notice its big feet and small ears. You would have to go to the Arctic to see one in the wild. It keeps to the icy coasts, and lives on its own, wandering across the sea ice in search of food. It is an excellent swimmer. It usually walks very slowly, with its head down and swinging from side to side. In winter, the females give birth to their cubs in dens dug in snowdrifts. They stay there until the weather becomes warmer and the cubs are large enough to leave.

Carnivore: Bear family
Length: 6–11 ft (1.8–3.4 m)
Feeds mainly on ringed seals, whale carcasses, fish, birds, berries, and grass
Tracks: 5 toes
Young: usually twins, every 2–3 years

Woodland Caribou
(Rangifer tarandus caribou)

Caribou are related to reindeer. Their fur is brownish and shaggy, with paler underparts, neck, and rump. Both males and females carry antlers, although the females' are smaller than the males'. Their wide hoofs stop them from sinking into the snow. Woodland caribou are found across the far north from Alaska to Newfoundland and Labrador, and south into the Rockies. They form large herds of up to 100,000 animals and are always on the move. In the rutting season, the bulls (males) gather harems of 12 to 15 cows (females). The calves are born between May and July, and are strong enough to follow the herd even before they are a day old. Some native peoples hunt caribou, not just for their meat, but also for their hides and other useful parts.

Ungulate: Deer family
Length: 6–8 ft (1.8–2.4 m),
Feeds on lichens, twigs, sedges, and fungi
Tracks: 2-toed rounded hoofs
Young: 1, sometimes 2, calves

Musk Ox
(Ovibos moschatus)

You cannot mistake a musk ox with its humped shoulders and long, dark hair which, in winter, reaches almost to the ground. Notice how its horns grow from a central base down each side of its face. You are most likely to see musk oxen in zoos, although they still live in the wild in the extreme north of Arctic Canada and Alaska. In winter, they are most likely to be seen on windswept hilltops where the snow has been blown away. They are active both day and night. In summer, musk oxen form small groups of up to 12 animals, and these join together to form larger herds of up to 100 in winter. If they are threatened, the adults form a defensive circle, each with their horns facing outward, and with the young calves protected in the center.

Ungulate
Length: 6–8 ft (1.8–2.4 m), of which tail is 2½–6½ in (6–17 cm)
Feeds on lichens, grasses, sedges, and other tundra plants
Tracks: 2-toed circular hoofs
Young: 1 calf every other year

Rivers & Waterways

The animals described in this section all live in or near fresh water. Some live among the sedges, reeds, and rushes that grow beside lakes, ponds, rivers, streams, and marshes. Look for their burrows in the banks.

Otters, minks, and beavers are well adapted to living in water but have to come to the surface to breathe. Their soft, thick fur keeps them warm and is protected by a layer of longer, waterproof "guard" hairs.

Beavers build their homes, called lodges, in water. They will pack twigs and branches with mud to build a dam across a stream to create a water-filled area large enough for a lodge. Once hunted nearly to extinction for their fur, beavers are now protected so that they are again becoming more widespread. The picture shows seven mammals from this section. How many can you recognize?

North American beaver, North American mink, muskrat, nutria, North American otter, swamp rabbit, water shrew.

Marsh Rice Rat
(Oryzomys palustris)

This rice rat, not a true rat, is very common in the southeastern United States as far north as New Jersey, but, since it is most active at night, you will rarely see it. It is grayish-brown above and paler below. It is smaller than a brown rat (see page 14), and has a longer tail. It lives in marshes and areas with sedges and grasses. It lives partly in water and partly on land, and builds a nest with grass and sedge in low bushes or rushes, or under debris. It also makes runways through the grass, and digs underground tunnels.

Rodent
Length: 7½–12 in (19–30 cm), of which half is the tail
Feeds on grains, seeds, plants, insects, and small crabs
Tracks: 4 toes on front, 5 toes on back feet
Young: several litters a year, each with 1–5 young

North American Mink
(Mustela vison)

You can tell that a mink belongs to the weasel family by its long body, short legs, small head, and long tail. It is larger than most other weasels, though smaller than the American marten and the fisher (see page 27). It has glossy brown fur. It is found over much of Canada and the United States, except in the deserts of the Southwest. Look for it in marshes, swamps, ponds, lakes, and rivers. It is an excellent swimmer and, in winter, it can swim under the ice, breathing from pockets of trapped air. It is most active at night, and lives on its own. Look for its den, which it digs into the bank of a stream or lake, and for its tracks in soft mud.

Carnivore: Weasel family
Length: 20–25 in (50–64 cm) excluding tail
Feeds on a wide variety of small land and water animals
Tracks: 5 toes
Young: 1 litter of 2–10 babies

North American Otter
(Lutra canadensis)

The North American otter is a type of river otter. It is much like a mink; however, its sleek brown fur is shorter than a mink's. It has webbed feet, and its long tail starts off broad and tapers to a point. Look for these otters along coastlines and in estuaries, as well as near lakes and streams. Sometimes they travel overland to get from one stream or lake to another. They often travel in pairs or family groups and are mainly active at night. They swim and dive through the water, and play on the riverbank. Look for slides in the mud or snow down to the water. They dig dens among the roots of shrubs or in the riverbank. (For sea otters, see p. 68.)

Carnivore: Weasel family
Length: 3–4½ ft (91–137 cm) including tail
Feeds on fish, water birds, small mammals, frogs, and shellfish
Tracks: 5 toes
Young: 1 litter of 2–3 babies

Water Shrew

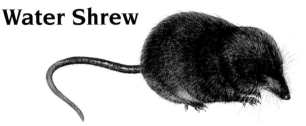

Insectivore
Length: up to 6 in (15 cm)
Feeds on earthworms, mayfly nymphs, and other small water creatures
Tracks: 5 toes
Young: more than 1 litter a year, each with 4 to 8 babies

(Sorex palustris)
Water shrews are smaller than rice rats and have darker fur. Their small ears are almost completely hidden in their fur. They are found throughout much of Canada and the United States, except in the Southeast and the Great Plains. Look for them in woodlands and marshes, near streams and rivers. They are extremely active, swimming and diving in the water. As they dive, their fur traps bubbles of air, so they seem to be covered in a silvery film. They can also run across the surface of the water. They make a nest of dried twigs, bark, and leaves among the plants and roots on the riverbank.

(Sylvilagus aquaticus)
Swamp rabbits are the largest cottontails. Their fur is yellow-brown, mottled with black on top and white below. Their tail is thin and slender and white underneath. Look for them in swamps and other wet ground in the southern United States from eastern Texas and Oklahoma to Georgia. Swamp rabbits are quite at home in water and swim well. They do not dig burrows but make their nests under logs or in a hollow in the ground. Sometimes they hide underwater with only their noses above the surface. Look for their droppings left on logs.

Swamp Rabbit

Rabbit and hare family
Length: 20–21 in (50–53 cm) in, of which tail is 2½ in (6 cm)
Feeds on plants, including water plants and crops
Tracks: 4 toes on front, 5 toes on back feet, which are much longer
Young: 2 litters, each with 1–5 babies

Muskrat
(Ondatra zibethicus)

A muskrat can be confused with a beaver, but it is smaller and its tail is much narrower and flattened vertically. It sometimes lives close to beavers, but normally builds its own similar-looking, but smaller winter lodge of grasses and sedges. It uses its lodge as a place to shelter and keep warm. It also digs a burrow into the bank which can be used by muskrats for many years and may have several different chambers. Muskrats are found all over North America, except in the southwest desert, parts of the southern United States, and the permanently frozen land of the Arctic. Wherever there are water and cattails, you are likely to see muskrats, even in developed areas. They like to feed on a flattened platform of vegetation, and here you can see the remains of their food.

Rodent—Length: 16–26 in (41–66 cm) including 10 in (2 cm) tail
Feeds mostly on water plants, but also clams, frogs, and fish
Tracks: 5 toes
Young: 1–3 litters, each with 1–11 babies

Nutria
(Myocastor coypus)

The nutria is also known as the coypu. They were introduced into North America from South America, and have now spread into swamps, marshes, ponds, and canals, particularly in southeastern states. To tell nutrias apart from beavers and muskrats, look at their tails. A beaver's tail is flattened into a paddle, a muskrat's is flattened vertically, while a nutria's is long and rounded. It is most active at night, and carries its food to a feeding station, which may be a log, brush, or other plants strong enough to hold the animal. It digs a burrow into the riverbank and often damages the sides of canals and streams. It is considered a pest in some areas because it feeds on local crops.

Rodent
Length: up to 40 in (100 cm), of which half is tail
Feeds on plants, both land and water
Tracks: 5-toed webbed feet
Young: 1 litter of 4–5 babies

North American Beaver
(Castor canadensis)

A beaver is large with dark brown to yellowish-brown fur, which looks black when wet. It has a broad, flat tail shaped like a paddle, which helps it to swim through the water. Listen for a loud crack as its slaps its tail on the water when it senses danger. Beavers used to be found in wetlands across North America, but are now rare in many areas, particularly in Florida and California. The best places to see them are in the northern national parks and refuges. They are most active at night but are sometimes seen during the day. Look for their dam built of mud and sticks across a stream or for their conical lodge built on the edge of or in a lake. Look, too, for the stumps of small trees which they have bitten through with their long front teeth and dragged to their home.

Rodent
Length: 3–4 ft (91–120 cm) including tail
Feeds on bark, twigs, and leaves
Tracks: 5-toed feet, front spread out, back webbed
Young: 1 litter of 1–8 babies

Detecting Rodents

Field voles, jumping mice, and harvest mice may be too fast and small for you to see, but you can look for their discarded food, runways, and nest holes. They are also a food source for other animals. You may find their bones in an owl pellet, for example.

Looking for tooth marks

Rodents have large front teeth that continue growing until the animal is old. The teeth do not get too large because they are constantly worn away as the animal chews. The next time you go walking in the countryside or in a park, look for chewed nuts and pine cones and chewed bark and roots of trees as well. Beavers sometimes gnaw right through tree trunks.

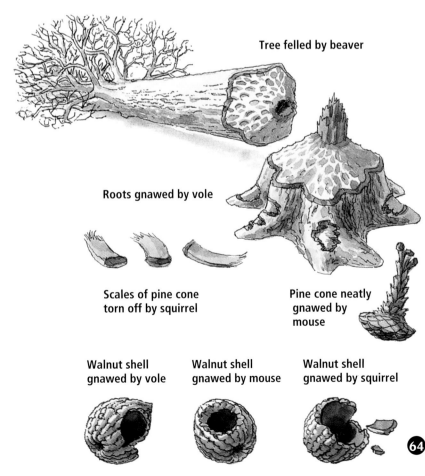

Tree felled by beaver

Roots gnawed by vole

Scales of pine cone torn off by squirrel

Pine cone neatly gnawed by mouse

Walnut shell gnawed by vole

Walnut shell gnawed by mouse

Walnut shell gnawed by squirrel

Winter home for harvest mice

If you live in the country, you may find harvest mice creeping into your garden to make a nest for the winter. Encourage them to come by providing a good home for them.

1 **Ask an adult to cut a slice off one side of an old tennis ball.**

Tunnels and runways

Most mammals follow a regular route as they forage. Rodents, such as voles and mice, and other small mammals, including shrews and moles, make runways through fallen leaves and among the grass. If you can follow them, these runways may lead to their nest. Look, too, for tunnels in the soft soil of riverbanks. If a hole is about 2 inches (5 centimeters) across, you can be sure it was made by a small rodent.

Moles stay underground, but if you find a small, cone-shaped mound of soil, clear it away and you will see its hole.

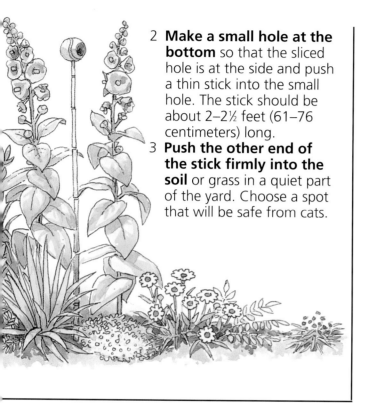

2 **Make a small hole at the bottom** so that the sliced hole is at the side and push a thin stick into the small hole. The stick should be about 2–2½ feet (61–76 centimeters) long.

3 **Push the other end of the stick firmly into the soil** or grass in a quiet part of the yard. Choose a spot that will be safe from cats.

3 **Lay out the bones.** Can you tell which bones they are? Can you find a jawbone with teeth?

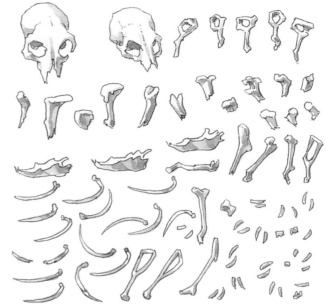

4 **Dispose of the gloves and bowl, and wash your hands with soap and water.**

Dissecting an owl pellet

Owls swallow their prey whole, but they cough up the parts they cannot digest in the form of a pellet. If you find an owl pellet—look under their roosts and feeding perches—put it in a plastic bag and take it home to examine it. Put on rubber gloves before handling the pellet.

1 **Soak the pellet for about an hour** in a disposable bowl of warm water.

2 **When the pellet is soft, again put on rubber gloves and move the pellet to an old newspaper.** Gently pull the pellet apart with tweezers or a small screwdriver.

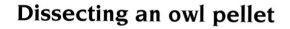

Coasts & Oceans

The sea can be a harsh place to live, especially when huge waves are whipped up by gales and storms. Some mammals go farther out to sea to find calmer water, while others come ashore or shelter in bays and harbors.

Apart from sea otters, most sea mammals have fins and flippers instead of legs. They swim under the water but have to come to the surface to breathe air. They have little or no hair on their skin, but instead have a thick layer of fat, called "blubber," to keep them warm.

Seals, sea lions, and walruses come ashore to give birth and look after their young. They form huge breeding colonies and return to the same grounds year after year. If you go to see one, be careful not to disturb the animals. Seals sometimes come ashore to rest on rocks and sandbanks.

Whales and dolphins stay farther out to sea and never leave the water. Many whales swim along the coasts of North America, as they migrate between the Arctic and the tropics. If you are lucky enough to see a school of whales swimming through the water, "blowing" out their damp, hot plumes of air, it is a sight you will never forget.

Unfortunately, sea mammals are still not safe from hunters. Young seals are covered with a soft fur called "lanugo." In spite of public protest many are killed for their fur. Norway and Japan still kill many thousands of minke whales each year. This picture shows six kinds of mammals from this section. How many can you recognize?

Common dolphins, sea otters, northern sea lions, gray whales, northern elephant-seal, Pacific white-sided dolphin.

Sea Otter
(Enhydra lutris)

Look for sea otters on the Pacific Coast of North America. A sea otter spends almost all of its life at sea, resting and feeding among masses of floating seaweed, called kelp. Its feet are webbed and are more like flippers than feet. Look for its long tail to tell it apart from seals. It likes to swim on its back, when you will see its grayish head and neck. It breaks open shellfish by smashing them against a rock held on its chest. It seldom comes ashore, except when there are severe storms. The pups are born at sea and can swim on their own by the time they are 2 months old. (For freshwater otters, see p. 61.)

Carnivore:
Weasel family
Length: 4–5 ft
(1.2–1.5 m)
Feeds on shellfish,
fish, and sea urchins
Young:
Usually 1 pup

Sea lions, walruses, and seals all have flippers instead of front and back legs. They have streamlined bodies and are well adapted to swimming, but like all sea mammals, they have to come to the surface to breathe in air. Watch for their heads bobbing up out of the water. They haul themselves on to land, both to rest and to breed, and this is the best time to see them.

Northern Sea Lion
(Eumetopias juatus)

You can tell a sea lion from a seal or walrus because you can see its ear flaps. Seals and walruses can hear too, but only a hole in their skin shows where their ears are. The northern sea lion, also known as Steller's sea lion, is common in the Pacific from California to Alaska. It is brownish or sometimes yellowish in color, and the bulls (males) are about three times as heavy as the cows (females). Soon after the pups are born, the bulls gather a harem (breeding group) of about 20 to 30 cows to breed again. If you see a sea lion at the zoo, notice how it turns its back flippers forward to help it walk on land.

Sea mammal: Sea lion family
Length: bulls about 9 ft (2.7 m), cows about 7 ft (2.1 m)
Feeds on fish and squid
Young: 1 pup

Californian Sea Lion
(Zalophus californianus)

Californian sea lions are the most familiar sea lions and the ones you are most likely to see at aquariums and marine parks. Listen for their constant, loud barking. Even in the wild they like to play and seem to be performing. Look for them on the Pacific Coast from Vancouver Island south to Baja California, Mexico. Californian sea lions are darker than northern sea lions. Look for their large eyes and small, pointed ears. They spend most of their time at sea, but are sometimes seen on rocky beaches. They are very sociable and gather in large colonies to breed. Each bull gathers a harem of cows.

Sea mammal:
Sea lion family
Length: bulls about 8 ft (2.4 m), cows about 6 ft (1.8 m)
Feeds on fish and squid
Young: 1 pup

Northern Fur Seal

Caribbean Manatee

Walrus

(Odobenus rosmarus)

You can easily identify a walrus from its long tusks—the largest have tusks up to 39 inches (99 centimeters) long. The walrus uses them for defense and to haul itself on to the ice. Walruses are found in the Arctic on both the Atlantic and Pacific coasts, but those in the West are larger than those in the East (they are sometimes found farther south). They are usually seen in groups along the edge of the ice pack.

Sea mammal: Walrus family
Length: 8–12 ft (2.4–3.7 m)
Feeds on shellfish gathered from the seabed
Young: 1 pup every other year

(Trichechus manatus)
The manatee likes warm waters and is found in estuaries and inlets from the Caribbean as far north as Florida and the Carolinas. Look for its broad head and thick lips. Only the front part can be seen out of the water, but you may see the rest of it in clear, shallow water. Look then for its broad, flattened tail. It has front flippers only and these are broad too, like paddles. It moves very slowly and cannot dive fast enough to escape danger—many have been killed or maimed by the propellers of power boats. They never leave the water, even to have their pups.

Sea mammal: Manatee family
Length: 13 ft (4 m)
Feeds on water plants
Young: 1 pup every 2–3 years

(Callorhinus ursinus)
Fur seals are closely related to sea lions and, like them, have visible external ears. They have long whiskers and a pointed snout. Males are blackish above and reddish below. Females are much smaller and grayer. Northern fur seals spend between six and eight months at sea. They can dive to depths of up to 450 feet to catch fish and squid, and swim up to 6,200 miles (10,000 kilometers) to their breeding grounds in the Bering Sea. Like other sea animals, many die because of oil spills and from swallowing plastic litter or becoming entangled in fishing nets.

Sea mammal: Sea lion family
Length: 4–7 ft (1.2–2.1 m)
Feeds on fish and squid
Young: 1 pup

Unlike fur seals, sea lions, and walruses, some seals cannot turn their back flippers forward to help them walk on land. They have to wriggle over the ground.

Ribbon Seal

Sea mammal: Seal family—Length: about 5½ ft (1.7 m)
Feeds on fish and squid—Young: 1 pup

(Phoca fasciata)
Ribbon seals (also known as banded seals) are rare, but if you saw one you would identify it quite easily from the bands of yellowish-white around its neck, front flippers, and rump. The rest of its fur is dark brown. It breeds only in the Arctic and comes no farther south than the drifting ice pack and the Alaskan Peninsula. It climbs up on to drifting ice to breed. Its pup is born on the ice in spring and is covered with white fur.

In North America, harp seals are found only in the Atlantic waters of the Arctic, as far south as Hudson Bay and the Gulf of St. Lawrence. The bulls are creamy-white or grayish with a black mark across their backs more or less in the shape of a harp. The cows are not so clearly marked. Harp seals can dive up to 900 feet (183 meters) in search of food and may swim many miles (or kilometers). However, they always keep fairly close to pack ice, and the young are born on the ice in February or March. There are far fewer harp seals than there once were. Harp seals are still hunted; the skins of both pups and adults are used for clothing and leather.

Harp Seal   *(Phoca groenlandicus)*

Sea mammal: Seal family
Length: 4½–6½ ft (1.3–2 m)
Feeds mostly on fish and shellfish—Young: 1 pup

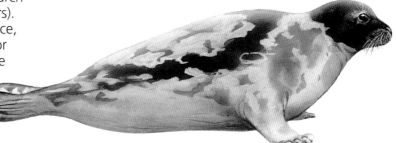

Hooded Seal

Sea mammal: Seal family—Length: 6–8 ft (1.8–2.4 m)
Feeds on fish and squid—Young: 1 pup

(Cystophora cristata)
Hooded seals get their name from a bag of skin on the bulls' heads, which they can inflate when angry to appear more fierce. Hooded seals range in color from silvery to bluish-gray, and they have dark patches scattered over the entire body. These seals live on the Atlantic side of the Arctic and are found between Baffin Island and the Gulf of St. Lawrence, but not in Hudson Bay. A bull mates with only one cow. The pup is born on ice toward the end of March.

Ringed Seal

(Phoca hispida)

This small seal looks much like a harbor seal but has white rings as well as dark spots on its gray back. It has brown whiskers and a catlike face. It is the most common seal in the Arctic and comes as far south as Newfoundland and Labrador, Hudson Bay, and Point Barrow in Alaska. When the sea is frozen over, the seal digs breathing holes in the ice with its flippers. Ringed seals live more or less on their own, except when they are breeding. When a cow is ready to give birth, she digs a large den for herself and her pup in a snowdrift. After the pup is born, she will sometimes move it from den to den to avoid predators.

Sea mammal: Seal family
Length: 3½ ft (1.1 m)
Feeds on small fish and shellfish—Young: 1 pup

Harbor Seal

(Phoca vitulina)

Harbor seals have a short, round head with a definite forehead, much like a dog's. They vary in color, but are usually yellowish-gray above with many dark blotches and streaks. You may see these seals close to the coast, in harbors, and in river estuaries on both the East and West coasts of North America. They come ashore to give birth, usually in early summer. The pup takes to the water often after only a few hours or a day or two.

Sea mammal: Seal family
Length: 4–5½ ft (1.2–1.7 m)
Feeds mainly on fish
and octopus
Young: usually 1 pup

Northern Elephant-seal

(Mirounga angustirostris)

This huge seal swims in the seas along the Pacific Coast from the Gulf of Alaska to Baja California, Mexico. It gets its name from its large size and from

Sea mammal:
Seal family
Length: bulls
about 20 ft (6.1 m),
cows 10–12 ft (3–3.7 m)
Feeds on small
sharks and other fish,
and squid
Young: 1 pup

the male's snout, which resembles an elephant's trunk. This seal comes ashore in December and January so that the cows (females) can give birth to the pups. The bulls (males) come first and establish a territory for their own harem (group of cows). Look for these seals on sandy shores, where they lie close together. You can tell which animals are the bulls. They are almost twice as big as the cows and in the breeding season they inflate their snouts to make them look bigger. The pups stay on land until they are about 5 months old.

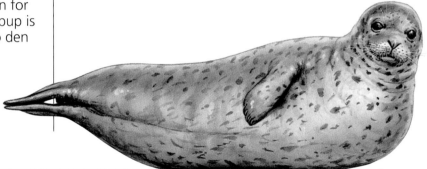

Dolphins, porpoises, and whales live entirely in the sea. They have no fur and their tails are horizontal, not vertical as with fish. Look for the notch in the middle of the tail. Like other sea mammals, they need to breathe air, which they do through blowholes on top of their heads. Both dolphins and porpoises sometimes follow ships, and this is probably the best way to get a good look at them in the wild.

Harbor Porpoise

(*Phocoena phocoena*)
Harbor porpoises are also known as common porpoises. They have no beak and are smaller and stouter than most dolphins. They are dark gray or black above and white below. You can see them on the Atlantic and Pacific coasts. They usually travel in small groups of 2 to 5 animals. Look for them in shallow waters near the coast and in estuaries, harbors, and rivers—watch for their black heads breaking the water to breathe. If you see one close up, look for the gray line from its jaws to its flippers.
Sea mammal: Dolphin family
Length: about 5½ ft (1.7 m)
Feeds on fish, shellfish, and squid
Young: 1 calf every year

Short-finned Pilot Whale
(*Globicephala macrorhynchus*)

This pilot whale is blackish all over, but the best way to recognize it is by its long, narrow flippers and bulging forehead. It may be seen on the Atlantic coast, as far north as New England, and on the Pacific coast up to Alaska. It usually swims in schools of 15 to 50 animals. In marine parks it can perform almost as well as a bottle-nosed dolphin.
Sea mammal: Dolphin family
Length: 14–21 ft (4–6 m)
Feeds mainly on squid
Young: 1 calf every 5–8 years

Pacific White-sided Dolphin
(Lagenorhynchus obliquidens)

Pacific white-sided dolphins have short, rounded snouts. Their backs are dark gray and they have white, gray, and yellow stripes down their sides. They are fast swimmers. Look for their dorsal fins cutting through the surface of the water. They swim close to the shore in winter, but farther out in summer. You may see them in large groups, often with seals and sea lions. They also like to ride the bow waves of ships. They are often seen in marine parks on the West Coast.
Sea mammal: Dolphin family
Length: about 8 ft (2.4 m)
Feeds on fish and squid
Young: 1 calf

Common Dolphin
(Delphinus delphis)

Common dolphins are smaller than many other dolphins and have a large "beak." They have black backs with white undersides and yellowish sides. They are very sociable and sometimes swim in large groups. They live in warm and temperate waters in both the Atlantic and Pacific oceans, usually keeping some distance from land, but you can also see them at marine parks throughout North America. In the wild, they like to ride the bow waves of ships and leap high out of the water.
Sea mammal: Dolphin family
Length: 6–8 ft (1.8–2.4 m)
Feeds on fish and squid
Young: 1 calf every 2–3 years

Bottle-nosed Dolphin
(Tursiops truncatus)

Sea mammal: Dolphin family
Length: up to 13 ft (4 m)
Feeds on fish and invertebrates from the seabed
Young: 1 calf every 3 years

Bottle-nosed dolphins are bluish-gray above and pale below. They have short beaks and jutting lower jaws. These are the dolphins most often seen in marine parks. They are slow swimmers, and they often leap clear out of the water. They swim in small groups, although they may form large schools of several hundred. They like to ride the bow waves of ships. They are the most common dolphin along the Atlantic coast. You may see them in coastal lagoons, bays, and sometimes in rivers on the Pacific as well as on the Atlantic coast.

Coasts & Oceans

Whales are related to dolphins and porpoises but are generally larger. There are two kinds of whales: baleen whales that filter the water through baleen (horny plates that hang from the upper jaw) to catch their food, and toothed whales that can bite their food. As a whale breathes out, it blows a cloud of mist into the air. You can identify a whale from the height and shape of its blow. Some whales, like bats, use a form of echolocation (see page 21) to help them detect rocks and other creatures in the water. They emit sounds and listen for their echoes bouncing off objects near them.

Blue Whale
(Balaenoptera musculus)

Blue whales are the largest animals ever known to have lived, and they are now very rare. They have been hunted almost to extinction and, like many other whales, are now protected. Blue whales are occasionally seen off the Atlantic and Pacific coasts and look very similar to fin whales. Their blow is almost vertical and may be as high as 29 feet (9 meters). They spend the summer in the cold Arctic waters feeding and move south to breed in warmer waters in the winter.

Sea mammal: Baleen whale
Length: about 100 ft (30 m)
Feeds on krill
Young: 1 calf every 2–3 years

Fin Whale
(Balaenoptera physalus)

This is the second largest kind of whale after the blue whale. It is sometimes called the common rorqual and is one of the rorquals most often seen. Rorquals are baleen whales that have long grooves on the throat and chest. Fin whales are shaped like torpedoes, are generally dark bluish-gray, and their small dorsal fins are set well back. They swim fast and lift their head and blowhole out of the water to breathe. Then they blow two to five tall spouts of mist before diving again. Sometimes they leap clear out of the water, falling back with a loud, belly-flopping crash. Look for them swimming close to land in spring, as they migrate from the warm waters of the South up to cold, food-laden waters of the North.

Sea mammal: Baleen whale—Length: up to 88 ft (27 m)
Feeds on plankton and fish
Young: 1 calf every 2–3 years

Minke Whale
(Balaenoptera acutorostrata)

The minke whale is the smallest rorqual. It is dark gray-black, but pale underneath, and often has a white band on the upper side of its flippers. It blows out five to eight low plumes that can be very hard to see. Minke whales are found in both the Atlantic and Pacific oceans. They swim closer to the coast than other baleen whales and are still hunted by Norwegian and Japanese whalers in spite of a worldwide ban. Some minke whales feed in winter in the cold, northern oceans, and in summer migrate south to the tropics to breed. They sometimes leap out of the water but dive back in headfirst with their tails arched.

Sea mammal: Baleen whale
Length: up to 33 ft (10 m)
Feeds on krill and fish
Young: 1 calf every
1 or 2 years

Gray Whale
(Eschrichtius robustus)

A gray whale has a narrow head and no fin on its back. When it blows, it makes several quick, low spouts. Both gray whales and humpback whales are often covered with barnacles. They rub themselves against underwater rocks to scrape the barnacles off. Like humpback whales, gray whales leap out of the water and are acrobatic swimmers. The best time to see them is between November and March. They breed in the waters around Baja California, then migrate to the northern Pacific and Arctic for the summer months. They are a big tourist attraction along the Pacific coast while they migrate.

Sea mammal: Baleen whale—Length: 43 ft (13 m)
Feeds on shellfish from seabed
Young: 1 calf every 2 or 3
years

Humpback Whale
(Megaptera novaeangliae)

A humpback whale has very long, narrow flippers and a small ridged fin, its "hump," set midway on its back. It swims slower than most other whales, but is very acrobatic. It jumps clean out of the water and slaps it with its flippers as it dives back in. Humpback whales live in every ocean and are often seen swimming along the coasts of North America, as they migrate between polar and tropical waters. They mate in the warmer waters. During this time, the males sing to attract the females and to keep the group together. The songs change over time.

Sea mammal: Baleen whale
Length: up to 62 ft (19 m)
Feeds on fish and krill
Young: 1 calf every 2 years

Black Right Whale
(Balaena glacialis)

This large, blackish whale has a big head and no fin on its back. Lumpy areas on the snout and chin and near the eyes are called callosities. When it blows, it produces two spouts in the shape of a V. It was called a right whale by whale hunters because it was the "right" whale to kill. It is also known as the northern right whale. It moves slowly through the water and does not sink when it is dead. Although they have been protected since 1937, their numbers are increasing only slowly. They can be found off both the Atlantic and Pacific coasts.

Sea mammal: Baleen whale
Length: about 55 ft (17 m)
Feeds on plankton
Young: 1 calf every
3–5 years

Sperm Whale
(Physeter macrocephalus)

Sperm whales are the largest toothed whales. They have very large, squarish heads and a low, thick fin on their back. It blows out an obvious, bushy plume from the tip of its head, which reaches up to 15 feet (5 meters) in front and to the left of it. It may blow up to 20 times before diving and can then stay underwater for over an hour. It has broad, triangular tail flukes, which it often throws high in the air as it starts its dive. Sperm whales can be seen off both the Atlantic and Pacific coasts of North America. They prefer warmer seas, although some mature males do migrate to polar seas in summer. Sperm whales usually live in groups of up to 50 animals. They are slow swimmers compared with other whales, and occasionally are still hunted for their meat and ambergris (a substance once used in the manufacture of some perfumes).

Sea mammal: Toothed whale
Length: up to 60 ft (18 m)
Feeds almost entirely on squid
Young: usually 1 calf about
every 4–6 years

Killer Whale
(Orcinus orca)

Probably the first sign of a killer whale would be its large dorsal fin slicing through the water (this triangular fin can be up to 6 feet [1.8 meters] high). You can tell this whale from a shark by its large size, black back, and white underside. Killer whales often swim in packs ranging from two to dozens of animals.
They sometimes
attack dolphins,
seals, and other
whales. It is
sometimes
called an orca.
Killer whales
are found in
all oceans.

Sea mammal: Toothed whale
Length: 20–30 ft (6–9 m)
Feeds mainly on fish and squid, but also on seals, sea lions, sea birds, penguins, and other whales
Young: 1 calf every 2–3 years

Narwhal
(Monodon monoceros)

Narwhals are easy to identify by the long tusk that sticks out from the front of the male's blunt head. The tusk, which is up to 8–9 feet (2.4–2.7 meters) long and twists in a spiral, is sometimes used for fighting. They are closely related to white whales, but their upper skin is heavily dappled with dark gray. Like the white whale, narwhals are found only along the cold Arctic coast.

Sea mammal: Toothed whale
Length: up to 17 ft (5.2 m) excluding tusk
Feeds on fish, squid, and shrimp
Young: 1 calf every 2–3 years

Beluga

(Delphinapterus leucas)
Belugas, also known as white whales, are relatively small and white or yellowish when mature. The young are dark gray. Belugas usually live in schools of between 5 and 30 animals, but sometimes several hundred group together. They do not move outside the cold waters of the Arctic and North Atlantic. Although commercial whaling of belugas has stopped, some are still hunted by the Inuit.

Sea mammal: Toothed whale
Length: about 15 ft (4.6 m)
Feeds on fish and shellfish mostly from seabed
Young: 1 calf every 3–4 years

Find Out More

Glossary

baleen plate: structure that some whales use to sieve the water for tiny shrimps and plankton

bat: only type of mammal that can fly

camouflage: coloration or other disguise that allows an animal to blend with its environment

carnivore: animal that eats mostly meat

desert: dry, barren area where only about half the ground has plant cover

dolphin: type of mammal that lives in the sea and never comes ashore

echolocation: using high-pitched sounds to locate food and avoid hitting things in the dark; bats use echolocation

gland: any of several small organs that control certain functions of the body; glands may produce milk, sweat, scent chemicals, or other substances

habitat: environment (area) that is the natural home of certain plants and animals

hibernate: to spend either a whole season or a period of severe weather in a state of deep sleep, especially one marked by a distinct lowering of metabolic rate and body temperature

insectivore: animal that eats mostly insects and other invertebrates

invertebrate: animal that does not have an internal backbone; this includes everything from plankton and worms to insects and lobsters

litter: family of young animals born together

mammal: warm-blooded animal that gives birth to live young (rather than laying eggs); newborn mammals drink their mothers' milk

plankton: tiny invertebrates that live in water—some whales feed on nothing but plankton

prairie: grasslands of central North America, stretching from the Appalachians to the Rockies

rodent: type of mammal that has large front teeth used for gnawing; these teeth never stop growing

roost: for a bird or bat, to sleep; or a sleeping or hibernating place

savanna: grassland that has a few trees and bushes and limited rainfall

seal: mammal that lives mostly in the sea, but comes ashore to breed and give birth

tragus: flap of skin on a bat that protects the entrance to the ear; the tragus also functions in echolocation

tundra: type of landscape that is often found between conifer forests and Arctic snows; the tundra is too cold and dry for trees to grow

ungulate: mammal with hoofs; ungulates have several stomach compartments and these help the animal to digest plant material

velvet: furry skin that covers a deer's antlers while the antlers grow

whale: type of mammal that lives in the sea and never comes ashore

Organizations

The **American Cetacean Society** is a good group to get information from if you are interested in whales and dolphins. Contact: American Cetacean Society, P.O. Box 1391, San Pedro, California 90733–1391; (310) 548-6279. http://www.acsonline.org

The **American Society of Mammalogists** accepts professional zoologists and serious amateurs as members. Write to: *Journal of Mammalogy,* Allen Marketing & Management, 810 East 10th Street, P.O. Box 1897, Lawrence, Kansas 66044-8897. http://www.mammalsociety.org

Bat Conservation International is interested in everything to do with bats and their preservation. Contact: Bat Conservation International, P.O. Box 162603, Austin, Texas 78716-2603; (512) 327-9721. http://www.batcon.org

In Canada, **Nature Canada** is a good starting point for information on mammals. Contact: Nature Canada, 85 Albert St., Suite 900, Ottawa, Ontario, K1P 6A4; (800) 267-4088. http://www.cnf.ca

For a complete listing of **U.S. National Wildlife Refuges,** contact: National Wildlife Refuge System, U.S. Fish & Wildlife Service; (800) 344-WILD. http://refuges.fws.gov

Many of the preserves owned by **The Nature Conservancy** and its chapters conserve unique and threatened habitats for mammals. Contact: The Nature Conservancy, 4245 North Fairfax Dr., Suite 100, Arlington, Virginia 22203–1606; (800) 628-6860. http://www.nature.org

If you are interested in wolves and in their conservation, contact the **Wolf Fund.** Write to: Wolf Fund, P.O. Box 471, Moose, Wyoming 83012.

Index

Additional Resources

Animal Habitats Tony Hare (Facts on File, 2001)
and ***Animal Life Cycles*** (2001).

DK Guide to Mammals Ben Morgan (DK
Publishing, 2003).

The Encyclopedia of Mammals David W.
MacDonald and Sasha Norris, eds. (Facts on File,
2001).

Grzimek's Encyclopedia of Mammals (5 volumes)
Bernhard Grzimek (Thomson-Gale, 2004).

Mammal Steve Parker (Dorling Kindersley, 2000).

Mammals (10 volumes) Pat Morris and Amy-Jane
Beer (Grolier, 2003).

***1000 Things You Should Know About
Mammals*** Duncan Brewer (Mason Crest, 2003).

Index

See *World Book's Science & Nature Guides Resources & Cumulative Index* volume for an explanation of the system used by scientists to classify living things.